SADLIER'S
New Parish Edition
Coming to Faith Program

COMING TO
GOD'S LIFE

Dr. Gerard F. Baumbach

Dr. Eleanor Ann Brownell

Moya Gullage

Helen Hemmer, I. H. M.

Gloria Hutchinson

Dr. Norman F. Josaitis

Rev. Michael J. Lanning, O. F. M.

Dr. Marie Murphy

Karen Ryan

Joseph F. Sweeney

with

Dr. Thomas H. Groome
Boston College

Official Theological Consultant
    Rev. Edward K. Braxton, Ph. D., S. T. D.

Scriptural Consultant
    Rev. Donald Senior, C. P., Ph. D., S. T. D.

Catechetical and Liturgical Consultants
    Dr. Gerard F. Baumbach
    Dr. Eleanor Ann Brownell

Pastoral Consultants
    Rev. Msgr. John F. Barry
    Rev. Virgilio P. Elizondo, Ph.D., S. T. D.

William H. Sadlier, Inc.
9 Pine Street
New York, New York 10005-1002

Contents

Unit 3   Sacraments of Healing and Service   page

DEAR YOUNG PEOPLE,

This book, **Coming to God's Life,** was written to help you understand more about the sacraments—the special ways we share in God's life and love.

In the sacraments, the Church recalls and carries on the work of Jesus Christ. You will learn that, through the sacraments, we are to become signs of God's love by welcoming, forgiving, healing, and serving others. We are to live as Jesus' disciples, sharing His good news with others.

When you use this book, ask the Holy Spirit to help you to:

- share more fully in the life and mission of the Church, especially in the celebration of the sacraments;
- celebrate the sacrament of the Eucharist weekly and Reconciliation regularly;
- discover ways that you can be a sign of God's love for your family, your friends, and your neighbors;
- learn to be like Jesus in His healing, forgiving service to everyone;
- imagine how Jesus wants you to continue His work and be a person of justice and peace.

All of us hope that you will enjoy learning about sharing God's life and love this year. Our prayer is that you will continue to grow as disciples of Jesus.

All of Us in the Sadlier Family

Called to Life

Our Life

Have you ever thought about your future? What kind of life do you want to have?

Take a few minutes now to write some key words that describe what your hopes are for your life.

Then write at least three qualities you have that will help you reach that goal.

Sharing Life

Join with a partner and share your ideas. Begin by making sure you know each other's name.

Listen carefully to each other. Maybe you can add to your partner's list of gifts and abilities. Sometimes people see gifts in us that we do not recognize in ourselves.

Then ask one another: What are God's hopes for your life?

Life in Its Fullness

Jesus once told this parable. His listeners did not understand it. Maybe you will.

I am the gate for the sheep. Whoever comes in by Me will be saved. The thief comes only to destroy. I have come in order that you might have life—life in all its fullness.

I am the good shepherd, who is willing to die for the sheep. When the hired man, who is not a shepherd, sees the wolf coming, he runs away and lets the wolf get the sheep. The hired man does not care about the sheep. I am the good shepherd. I know My sheep and they know Me.

From John 10:7–15

What does this parable say about Jesus' love for us?

Jesus, our Good Shepherd, wants us to "have life." He was willing even to die that we might have fullness of life.

This year we will explore together the life that Jesus Christ came to give us. We will learn how this life can be nourished and grow through the life-giving sacraments of the Church.

We will share the life of faith among ourselves and find ways to reach out to others so they, too, may have "life in all its fullness."

We will identify and fight against all those things that threaten Christ's life in us—the "thieves" and "wolves" of falsehood, abuse, violence, indifference, and irresponsibility.

Take a few minutes now to look through your new book *Coming to God's Life*. Share together what lesson you are most looking forward to studying this year.

COMING TO FAITH

Play a word association game. Take turns saying what words or pictures come to mind when you hear the word *life*. Have someone write the ideas on newsprint or the board as they are given.

Choose the word or picture that says best what life means to you. In the space above, create a personal symbol or logo that illustrates it.

During the year, you might want to look back occasionally at this page to see whether your thoughts about life have changed.

PRACTICING FAITH

With your friends in a prayer circle, hold your *Coming to God's Life* book. Go around the circle, each one saying: "My name is .... This year I hope to grow in God's life by...."

† Close by praying the Our Father together.

Talk with your catechist about ways you and your family might use the "Faith Alive" pages together. You might especially want to do the Good Shepherd activity with a family member.

10

This year your son or daughter will explore what Jesus meant when He said that He had come "to bring life—life in all its fullness" (John 10:10). He or she will learn how as Catholics we are called to live a sacramental life, a life ever alert to a special awareness of God's presence in the ordinary things and events of life. This awareness is the basis of the seven sacraments that we celebrate as Catholics.

In the seven sacraments, the Church recalls and carries on the work of Jesus Christ in our world. Your child will learn how we are to become life-giving signs ourselves—signs of God's life by becoming people who welcome, forgive, heal, and serve others. You can participate in this process by talking with your child about these things and by growing with your child in God's life. Here are some ways *Coming to God's Life* can assist you.

■ Talk about each lesson together, including the pictures and artwork, if possible, since they are an essential part of the program. Encourage a conversation about the *Faith Summary* statements. The symbol reminds you to help your child learn the *Faith Summary* statements by heart. Remember that "learning by heart" includes, but means much more than, memorization. It means taking and making these convictions one's own, making them part of one's heart. You will support this "learning by heart" by talking about the *Faith Summary* statements with your fifth grader. Some you may repeat a number of times to commit to memory, but be sensitive about this; not everyone has equal facility with memorization. It is much more important that a person have them in his or her heart, rather than being able to repeat the statements exactly.

■ Invite your son or daughter to share with you any songs or experiences of prayer that have been learned or shared. Even before truths of our Catholic faith are fully understood, they can be appropriated through a favorite song or prayer.

■ Use the *Faith Alive at Home and in the Parish* pages (this is the first of them) to continue and to expand your child's catechesis through the experience of the community of faith in your family and in the parish family. There will be a variety of activities on these pages. Try to do at least one with your fifth grader.

The **Family Scripture Moment** is offered as a unique opportunity for the family to share faith by "breaking open" God's word in the Bible together. The "moment" can be as brief or as long as you wish. The following simple outline is one way to use this time together.

■ **Gather** together as a family. All can participate from the youngest to the oldest.

■ **Listen** to God's word as it is read, slowly and expressively, by a family member.

■ **Share** what you hear from the reading that touches your own life. Give time for each one to do this.

■ **Consider** the points suggested as a way to come to a deeper understanding of God's word.

■ **Reflect** on and then share any new understandings.

■ **Decide** as a family ways you will try to live God's word.

In this fifth-grade text, selected passages from the Gospel of John will be suggested for family faith sharing, prayer, and reflection.

Learn by heart Faith Summary

- Jesus Christ is our Good Shepherd.
- Jesus came to bring us life—life in all its fullness.

The Good Shepherd

In the parable Jesus talks about the good shepherd who will give his life for the sheep. He also talks about "thieves" and "wolves" who bring death. What things in your life can you recognize as dangers to God's life in you? How can you protect yourself from these dangers?

Review

Take a few moments to go over the *Faith Summary* together. Ask your fifth grader to tell you the parable of the Good Shepherd. Encourage him or her to learn the summary by heart.

Play a word game with your family. Take turns finishing this sentence and explaining your choice.

FAMILY SCRIPTURE MOMENT

Gather and invite family members to recall their favorite teacher. Ask: What did you admire about this teacher? Then **Listen** as a family as Jesus invites us to "Come and see."

Upon seeing Jesus, John the Baptist said, "There is the Lamb of God!" Two disciples heard him say this and went with Jesus. Jesus turned, saw them following Him, and asked, "What are you looking for?" They answered, "Where do You live, Rabbi?" (This word means "Teacher.") "Come and see," He answered. So they went with Him and saw where He lived, and spent the rest of that day with Him.

From John 1:35–39

Share what kind of teacher you think Jesus was and how He taught best.

Consider for family enrichment:

◼ As John's Gospel begins, John the Baptist serves as a witness, identifying Jesus as the Lamb of God. Two of John's disciples immediately follow Jesus, giving Him the honored title of "rabbi," or teacher.

◼ By our sharing of God's word, we also accept Jesus' invitation and are ready to learn from Him, our best teacher.

Reflect and **Decide** What do we as a family hope to learn from Jesus the teacher this year? As a family, how will we show that we follow Jesus this week?

1 ⊥ Jesus Christ Reveals God

Our Life

Someone once said that "a picture is worth a thousand words." See how well you can "read" the pictures on this page. What do they tell you about the ways God is with us in our world today?

What does God mean to you?

Sharing Life

Help one another remember what you know about Jesus that shows

- He is divine—God's own Son;
- He is human—as we are.

Imagine some things that Jesus can teach you about yourself.

OUR CATHOLIC FAITH

Jesus Is Human

We first learned about Jesus as small children when someone told us the Christmas story. We know that Jesus was born in a stable at Bethlehem because there was no room for Mary and Joseph in the inn.

As we got older we learned from other gospel stories how much Jesus was like us. Jesus got tired. He felt thirsty and hungry. Jesus loved and obeyed His parents. He enjoyed doing things with His friends. He prayed and worshiped in the synagogue. Jesus was like us in every way except one—He never sinned. He was tempted, but He always said no to sin.

This story helps us to remember how human Jesus was.

Among Jesus' closest friends were a man named Lazarus and his two sisters, Martha and Mary.

One day Lazarus became sick and was dying. Martha and Mary sent for Jesus, but by the time Jesus arrived, Lazarus had died.

When Jesus saw Mary and Martha crying, He felt very sad and began to cry, too. He felt as we do when someone we love dies.

From John 11:1–44

Jesus also faced death as all people do. In His suffering and death, Jesus was truly one of us.

Jesus Is Divine

Jesus is one of us, but He is also the Son of God. This is what we mean when we say that Jesus is divine.

In the Creed at Mass, we say that Jesus is "one in Being with the Father." This means "Jesus is true God." Here is one of the stories from the gospels that tells how the disciples began to learn that Jesus was God's own Son.

One day Jesus was in a boat on the lake of Galilee with His disciples. Jesus was sleeping when a fierce storm suddenly started. The disciples were so scared that they woke Jesus, yelling, "Save us, Lord! We are about to die!"

"Why are you so frightened? What little faith you have," Jesus answered. Then He got up and commanded the winds and the waves to stop, and there was a great calm. The disciples were amazed. Jesus had done something only God can do.

From Matthew 8:23–27

Like the disciples in the boat, we turn in prayer to Jesus for help. Because Jesus is really one of us, we know that He always understands how we feel. Because He is the Son of God, He can always help us.

A **disciple** is one who learns from and follows Jesus Christ.

Jesus showed us who God is more clearly than anyone had ever done before. John, one of Jesus' closest friends, used three words to tell what he had learned about God from Jesus. He wrote, "God is love" (1 John 4:8).

Jesus showed us that God is love. Jesus cared for the rich and the poor, the healthy and the sick, saints and sinners. He showed us how to work for justice and peace. Jesus still works through us and through others to show God's love in the world.

COMING TO FAITH

How would you explain to a friend that Jesus is both human and divine?

Complete the following sentences.

Because Jesus wept when His friend Lazarus died, I know that....

Because Jesus calmed the storm at sea, I know that....

Because Jesus' love for us will never end, I know that God....

Because Jesus worked for justice and peace, we should....

PRACTICING FAITH

Gather quietly in a circle. Imagine that Jesus is with you in the center of the circle. After a minute, read aloud each of the following situations. Take turns going to the center of the circle and responding to each situation the way you think Jesus would want.

● I have a lot of trouble getting along with my brother or sister. Jesus says....

● It really bothers me that I am not good at sports (or schoolwork). Jesus says....

● Sometimes I feel sad and alone. Jesus says....

● Some people think the best way to solve problems is through fighting. Jesus says....

● I feel a friend has really betrayed me. Jesus says....

† Pray together: Jesus, help us to be more like You. Help us to show God's love to others so that all will know that we are Your disciples.

Talk with your catechist about ways you and your family can use the "Faith Alive" pages together. You might ask a family member to do the Incarnation activity with you.

FAITH ALIVE AT HOME AND IN THE PARISH

This lesson deepened your fifth grader's understanding that Jesus is both human and divine. That the divine nature and a human nature existed together in the one person of Jesus Christ is a central doctrine of the Christian faith. This doctrine that the Son of God took on a human nature gives us hope in God's overwhelming love for us.

Knowing that Jesus is one of us helps us to turn to Him more readily and to try to live as He did. You can lead your son or daughter to an appreciation of God's love by providing an experience of a family trying to live as Jesus did.

Ask yourself:
■ *Do my daily actions show my family God's love for them?*
■ *What will my family and I do this week to show we believe that God's love is present in each of us? in our friends? in the poor?*

To help your fifth grader grow in his or her understanding that Jesus is like us and that we can imitate Him, do the activity together.

† Family Prayer

O loving God, You showed Your great love for us by sending Your Son into the world. May we truly know and experience Your love in our family. Help us to love one another as You love us. Amen.

Learn by heart Faith Summary

● Jesus Christ is both human and divine.

● Jesus showed us that "God is love" by the things He said and did.

● God works through us and others to show God's love in the world.

Describing the Incarnation

The Son of God became one of us. This is called the incarnation. The word *incarnation* means "became flesh." The incarnation is the mystery of God becoming one of us in Jesus Christ.

Describe:

one way Jesus was like us.

_____

_____

one way you will try to be like Jesus.

_____

_____

Review

Before doing this *Review*, have your fifth grader go over the *Faith Summary*. Encourage him or her to learn the first two statements by heart. The answers to numbers 1–4 appear on page 216. The response to number 5 will help you see how well your fifth grader understands that God's love is present in our lives. When the *Review* is completed, go over it together.

Circle the letter beside the correct answer.

1. In His suffering and death, Jesus showed us that He was truly
   a. weak.
   b. divine.
   c. human.
   d. none of the above

2. Jesus' miracles reveal that He is
   a. a magician.
   b. divine.
   c. human.
   d. none of the above

3. Jesus taught us that God
   a. is love.
   b. never forgives.
   c. has a white beard.
   d. is kind some of the time.

4. God loves and cares for
   a. the rich and poor.
   b. the healthy and sick.
   c. saints and sinners.
   d. all of the above.

5. How will you show you believe that God's love is present in your life?

   _____

   _____

FAMILY SCRIPTURE MOMENT

Gather and ask: Do we sometimes feel that we have lost our way in life? What do we do to get back on track? Then **Listen** as Jesus shows us the way.

"Do not be worried and upset," Jesus told His disciples. "There are many rooms in my Father's house, and I am going to prepare a place for you. And after I go and prepare a place for you, I will come back and take you to Myself. You know the way that leads to the place where I am going." Thomas said, "Lord, we do not know where You are going; so how can we know the way to get there?" Jesus answered him, "I am the way, the truth, and the life; no one goes to the Father except by Me."

From John 14:1–6

Share what each person heard from Jesus in this reading.

Consider for family enrichment:

■ John's Gospel emphasizes the intimate relationship between Jesus the Son and God the Father. Jesus promises His disciples that He is the way to the Father.

■ By following Jesus, we will come to share in all He has prepared for us in heaven.

Reflect and **Decide** How can we as a family be more faithful to the way of Jesus? Pray together: Jesus, help us to follow You as the way, the truth, and the life.

Jesus, help us to be messengers of Your life to others—life in all its fullness.

OUR LIFE

GOOD NEWS BULLETINS

Join us after 8 A.M. Mass. We need helpers to make sandwiches for our "special guests," the homeless.

Environment Guardians: Meet at 9 A.M. Saturday for beach and street cleanup. Bring plastic bags!

Thanks to all the fifth and sixth graders who visited the nursing home last week. Everyone wants you to come back!

Can you add a bulletin about something you have done or might do to bring good news to others?

SHARING LIFE

Share your ideas about what might be the very best "good news" our human family could hear.

Make a list of your ideas and try to come to agreement about the best "good news" of all. Talk about what you can do to make it happen.

The Kingdom of God

The best news we can hear is that God loves us and cares deeply about us—no matter what. God gave us Jesus to show us that God loves us and will always love us. This is the very best "good news" that Jesus came to share with us.

When Jesus was about thirty years old, He began His ministry of preaching the good news of God's love. He did this in word and action. He healed the sick. He helped the poor, fed the hungry, and forgave sinners. The people began to realize that Jesus was someone very special.

Just about the time Jesus began His work among the people, a prophet was telling everyone that the Messiah, or Savior, was coming soon. The prophet's name was John the Baptist.

One day some of John's followers came to see Jesus and asked whether He was the Promised One, the Messiah.

In response, Jesus pointed out the special things He was doing: "The blind can see, the lame can walk, those who suffer from dreaded skin diseases are made clean, the deaf can hear, the dead are raised to life, and the good news is preached to the poor."

From Luke 7:18–22

Jesus was saying that His words and actions were the very things the Messiah, the Promised One of God, would say and do. Jesus Christ was the Messiah. He lived His whole life for the kingdom, or reign, of God.

Living the Good News

Jesus invites all people to live for the kingdom of God. In the Our Father Jesus taught us to pray "Thy kingdom come; thy will be done on earth as it is in heaven"

FAITH WORD

The **kingdom**, or **reign**, **of God** is the saving power of God's life and love in the world.

(from Matthew 6:9–14). We are to share in Jesus' work of bringing about God's reign on earth by living as disciples of Jesus.

There are times when we do not live the good news of God's love. We fail to love others as we should. We fail to do the things that bring God's justice and peace. These things keep us from living for God's reign. Because of our sins, the reign of God is not yet complete.

There are many ways that we can live for God's reign. These include carrying an elderly person's bundles, cleaning up a messy room without being asked, or saying no to cheating. All these are ways of doing God's loving will for us.

We build the reign of God every time we try to be just, or treat others fairly, and work to be peacemakers. Living in God's reign also means helping everyone to know and share in God's life and love.

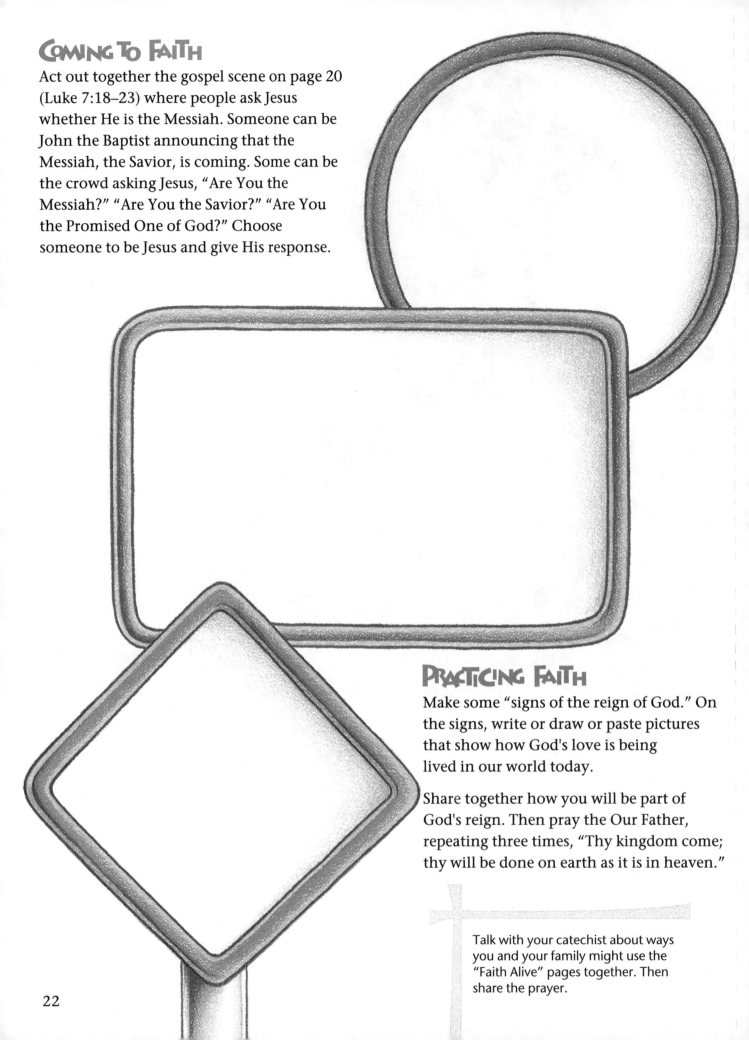

Coming To Faith

Act out together the gospel scene on page 20 (Luke 7:18–23) where people ask Jesus whether He is the Messiah. Someone can be John the Baptist announcing that the Messiah, the Savior, is coming. Some can be the crowd asking Jesus, "Are You the Messiah?" "Are You the Savior?" "Are You the Promised One of God?" Choose someone to be Jesus and give His response.

Practicing Faith

Make some "signs of the reign of God." On the signs, write or draw or paste pictures that show how God's love is being lived in our world today.

Share together how you will be part of God's reign. Then pray the Our Father, repeating three times, "Thy kingdom come; thy will be done on earth as it is in heaven."

Talk with your catechist about ways you and your family might use the "Faith Alive" pages together. Then share the prayer.

In this lesson, your fifth grader continued to learn more about the reign of God. Although the kingdom has already come in Jesus, it is also a future reality that will only be completed at the end of time. As the Lord's Prayer teaches, it begins on earth and is completed in heaven. Jesus founded the Church to proclaim the good news of the kingdom of God. From its beginning, the Church contained the seed of the kingdom of God. (See Luke 12:32.) The Church is an instrument of the kingdom and helps us to live for it. Your son or daughter has learned that to live for the reign of God includes trying each day as hard as we can to love God, our neighbors, and ourselves. This includes living justly and being peacemakers. To help your family understand this, talk about the greatest of all the commandments, the Law of Love.

The Law of Love
"Love the Lord your God with all your heart, with all your soul, and with all your mind. Love your neighbor as you love yourself. This is the greatest commandment of all."
From Matthew 22:34–40

Decide what you and your family will do to live the Law of Love so that you might help to bring about the reign of God. Then do the activity.

† Family Prayer

As a family say the Our Father to pray for the kingdom of God. Close your eyes and imagine both what God wants the reign of God to be and how God wants you to live. (This kind of prayer is called meditation.)

Then pray aloud:
"Thy kingdom come; thy will be done on earth as it is in heaven."

Learn by heart Faith Summary

- Jesus announced the good news of the kingdom, or reign, of God. The good news is that God loves us and will always love us.

- The reign of God is the saving power of God's life and love in the world.

- Jesus lived His whole life for the reign of God and calls us to do the same.

Living the Law of Love as a Family
We all like to be told how well we are doing. Write a congratulations card to someone in your family when you see the Law of Love in action.

Review

Before doing this *Review*, have your fifth grader go over the *Faith Summary*. Encourage him or her to learn the first two statements by heart. The answers to numbers 1–4 appear on page 216. The response to number 5 will show how well your fifth grader is learning to live for the reign of God. When the *Review* is completed, go over it together.

Circle the letter beside the correct answer.

1. Jesus announced the good news that
   a. He would conquer the Romans.
   b. God would make the apostles great rulers.
   c. God loves us.
   d. the Romans would leave Palestine.

2. Jesus pointed to His words and deeds to show that He was
   a. a foreigner.
   b. the Messiah.
   c. an Egyptian.
   d. a Palestinian.

3. Jesus came to
   a. bring about the reign of God.
   b. preach the good news.
   c. help us do God's loving will.
   d. all of these

4. We live for the reign of God by
   a. thinking only of ourselves.
   b. loving only those people who are kind to us.
   c. living the Law of Love.
   d. rejecting the poor.

5. How will you try to live for the reign of God this week?

   _____

   _____

   _____

FAMILY SCRIPTURE MOMENT

Gather and recall times when family or friends have been seriously ill. Did you turn to God for help? Then **Listen** to a healing story from John's Gospel.

Near the Sheep Gate in Jerusalem there is a pool. A large crowd of sick people were lying on the porches. A man was there who had been sick for thirty-eight years. Jesus saw him lying there, so He asked him, "Do you want to get well?" The man answered, "Sir, I don't have anyone here to put me in the pool when the water is stirred up; while I am trying to get in, somebody else gets there first." Jesus said to him, "Get up, pick up your mat, and walk." Immediately the man got well.
From John 5:2–9

Share Imagine and discuss how Jesus felt and why He was prompted to heal this sick person.

Consider for family enrichment:

■ By healing the paralytic at a pool that had a reputation for its healing waters, Jesus gave a sign that the reign of God had come in Him.

■ We, too, can turn to Jesus for healing and courage in times of illness and suffering.

Reflect and **Decide** How will we respond to people who are sick and disabled in our own family and in our parish?

3 Jesus Christ Blesses Our Lives

Lord Jesus,
make us
instruments of
Your peace.

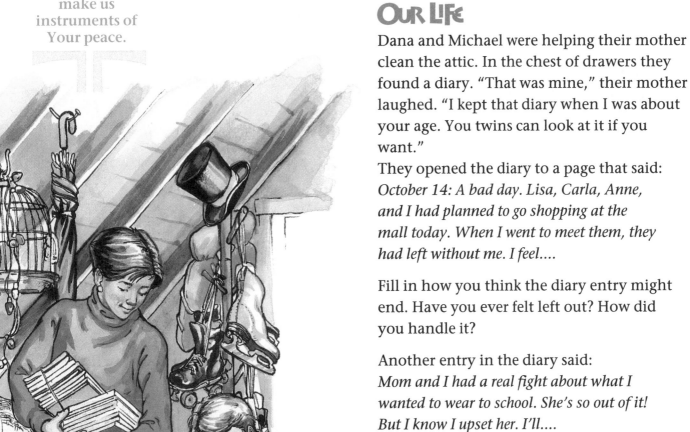

OUR LIFE

Dana and Michael were helping their mother clean the attic. In the chest of drawers they found a diary. "That was mine," their mother laughed. "I kept that diary when I was about your age. You twins can look at it if you want."

They opened the diary to a page that said:
October 14: A bad day. Lisa, Carla, Anne, and I had planned to go shopping at the mall today. When I went to meet them, they had left without me. I feel....

Fill in how you think the diary entry might end. Have you ever felt left out? How did you handle it?

Another entry in the diary said:
Mom and I had a real fight about what I wanted to wear to school. She's so out of it! But I know I upset her. I'll....

Complete the entry. What do you usually do to make up?

SHARING LIFE

Share together:

● why we should make people feel welcome and included in a group.

● how we can solve problems that separate us without hurting one another.

25

An Invitation to All

Jesus chose disciples from among people left out by other people in society. His friends included women, tax collectors, poor people, and sinners. This may not seem strange to us, but in Jesus' time it was unusual.

Jesus was most interested in the people society ignored. He worked to change unjust or unfair attitudes and practices.

Here is a Bible story of Jesus reaching out to one of the Jewish people's greatest enemies, their Roman conquerors.

One day a Roman soldier said to Jesus, "Sir, my servant is sick in bed at home, unable to move, and suffering terribly."

Jesus immediately said, "I will go and make him well."

Surprised that Jesus would actually go to his house, the officer blurted out, "I am not worthy to have you come into my house. Only speak the word, and my servant will get well."

Amazed by this Roman's faith, Jesus turned to the people watching Him and said, "I tell you, I have never found anyone in Israel with faith like this. I assure you that many will come from the east and the west and sit down at the feast in the kingdom of heaven."

From Matthew 8:5–11

By healing the Roman officer's servant, Jesus showed that all people are welcome in the reign of God.

Kingdom of heaven is another way of saying kingdom of God in Matthew's Gospel.

Jesus, Healer and Forgiver

Besides physical healing, there is another kind of healing, a spiritual healing. It is called forgiveness. Forgiveness heals the separation from God and from others that sin causes.

For Jesus, forgiveness of sins was even more important than physical healing. Jesus, our Savior, reached out to heal the separation brought about by sin. He forgave sinners and reconciled them with God.

Even as He was dying on the cross, Jesus forgave those who crucified Him. He said, "Forgive them, Father! They don't know what they are doing" (Luke 23:34).

Like Jesus, we try to forgive those who hurt us, no matter how great the hurt. When we have been the ones who have hurt another person, we must try to tell the person that we are sorry and ask for forgiveness.

Jesus will help us to be friends again. He wants us to live in peace with all people. This is how we do God's loving will for us and live for the reign of God.

27

Coming to Faith

Here are some role-playing situations to do with your friends to help you understand welcoming, healing, forgiveness, and reconciliation. Divide into groups and act out what might be said and done.

● Mike is coming back to school after a battle with cancer. He is anxious about it because he looks so different. His hair has not grown back yet and he is very thin. How will people react to him?

● Meg and Brittany have been arguing and fighting together. They say they hate each other. Friends decide to bring them together and try to solve the problem.

● A new boy has just joined your class. He seems to want to be by himself and be unfriendly.

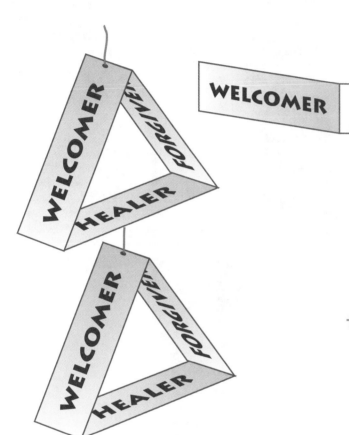

WELCOMER HEALER FORGIVER

Practicing Faith

Take a strip of paper (10" x 2"). On one side write one of these words: welcomer, healer, or forgiver. On the back put one thing you will do this week to be the kind of person who lives for the reign of God.

†Now gather in a prayer circle. Quietly link your strip of paper with those of the people on either side. When the chain is complete, pray as follows:

● *The "welcomers" pray*: Jesus, Your love and care went out to everyone. Help us to be welcomers in Your name.

● *The "healers" pray*: Jesus, help us to be healers by speaking and acting kindly.

● *The "forgivers" pray*: Jesus, You forgave even those who put You to death. Teach us how to mend the things that separate us.

All hold the chain up high and pray the Prayer of Saint Francis (page 29).

Talk with your catechist about ways you and your family can use the "Faith Alive" pages. Perhaps you can read together from the Bible the Sermon on the Mount and talk about some of the teachings of Jesus.

FAITH ALIVE

AT HOME AND IN THE PARISH

In this chapter your fifth grader has learned more about the ways Jesus showed us to live for the reign of God. Jesus welcomed everyone, helped the poor, healed the sick, and showed us how to forgive. To know Jesus Christ is to recognize how central to His identity are the ministries of hospitality, healing, forgiveness, and reconciliation. Jesus constantly extended His friendship to sinners, to the poor, to the outcasts. As His followers, we are called to continue His mission of healing and reconciliation.

The Sermon on the Mount contains a summary of many of Jesus' teachings about living for the reign of God. You may wish to read together part of the Sermon on the Mount (Matthew 5:1–7:29). Then do the activity with your son or daughter. In the space below write, draw, or paste one thing that Jesus taught in the Sermon on the Mount that you will try to do with your family before the next lesson.

† Family Prayer

Pray this prayer of Saint Francis after your evening meal.

Lord, make me an instrument of Your peace:
where there is hatred, let me sow love;
where there is injury, pardon;
where there is doubt, faith;
where there is despair, hope;
where there is darkness, light;
where there is sadness, joy.
Grant that I may not so much seek to be consoled as to console, to be understood as to understand, to be loved as to love.

Learn by heart Faith Summary

- Jesus invited everyone to live for the reign of God.

- Forgiveness heals the separation from God and from others that sin causes.

- Like Jesus, we try to forgive those who hurt us, no matter how great the hurt.

Living the Sermon on the Mount

Forgive • Love • Have Faith • Share

Review

Before doing this *Review*, have your fifth grader go over the *Faith Summary*. Encourage him or her to learn the second and third statements by heart. The answers to numbers 1–4 appear on page 216. The response to number 5 will show how well your fifth grader is trying to be fair and just to family and to others. When the *Review* is completed, go over it together.

Circle the letter beside the correct answer.

1. Jesus' healing of the Roman's servant showed that
   a. He was afraid of the Romans.
   b. faith is not important.
   c. all are welcome in God's reign.
   d. He obeyed the orders of the Romans.

2. Forgiveness heals the separation from God and others caused by
   a. friendship.
   b. sin.
   c. love.
   d. reconciliation.

3. Besides healing people's bodies, Jesus
   a. said they would never be sick again.
   b. reconciled them to God.
   c. forgave their sins.
   d. both b and c

4. Like Jesus, we try to forgive
   a. all those who hurt us.
   b. no one who hurts us.
   c. some of those who hurt us.
   d. only those who say "I'm sorry."

5. What will you do to be fair to another person this week?

_____

_____

FAMILY SCRIPTURE MOMENT

Gather and invite family members to recall times when friends turned away from them or refused their invitations and tell how they felt. Then **Listen** to Jesus at a time when many of His followers had found His teaching on the Bread of Life "too hard."

Because of this, many of Jesus' followers turned back and would not go with Him any more. So He asked the twelve disciples, "And you—would you also like to leave?" Simon Peter answered Him, "Lord, to whom would we go? You have the words that give eternal life. And now we believe and know that You are the Holy One who has come from God."

From John 6:66–69

Share Ask: What do you think of Peter's response? If you had been there, how would you have responded?

Consider for family enrichment:

■ After Jesus told the crowd that His own Body and Blood would be their source of everlasting life, many turned away from Him. But the apostle Peter proclaimed the disciples' faith in Jesus.

■ Like Peter, we accept Jesus' invitation to remain with Him and live for God's reign.

Reflect and **Decide** How might we extend Jesus' invitation to others—especially those who may feel left out of parish life?

4 The Church Carries on Jesus' Mission

Our Life

While Jesus was on earth, He had many disciples. Let's see how some of them might be described.

Peter—a rough, uneducated fisherman. He was good-hearted but often boastful. Jesus saw special qualities in Peter. He made Peter the leader.

Martha—sometimes worried too much about everyday cares. But she was one of the first disciples to recognize Jesus as the Messiah and Son of God.

Thomas—often called "Doubting" Thomas, because for him only "seeing was believing." He wouldn't accept Jesus' resurrection until he could actually touch Him.

Mary Magdalene—described in the gospels as a helper of Jesus. With other women disciples, she stood at the foot of Jesus' cross and was one of the first to hear the good news of His resurrection.

These are just some of the disciples of Jesus. Why do you think they followed Him?

How would you describe yourself as a disciple of Jesus?

Sharing Life

Discuss together: Why is it sometimes difficult to work with other people? When is it easy?

Are there things in our Church or society that sometimes make it difficult for people to work together?

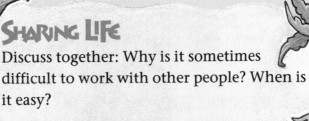

31

The Church Welcomes

Jesus knew His disciples would need help to build up His Church. He promised to send them the Holy Spirit. God the Holy Spirit is the third Person of the Blessed Trinity. After Jesus' ascension into heaven, the disciples were praying together with Mary. Suddenly they heard a strong wind. Then they saw what looked like tongues of fire settling over the heads of each one. They were filled with the Holy Spirit, as Jesus had promised. This happened on Pentecost, the day the Church celebrates the coming of the Holy Spirit.

The disciples, who were once afraid, were now full of courage. The Holy Spirit helped them to come out from behind locked doors and to preach the good news of Jesus to everyone.

From Acts 2:1–13

The disciples invited and welcomed all people into the community of Jesus' followers, the Church.

Today the mission of the Church is to teach Jesus' good news and way of life to all.

As Catholics we teach the good news when we welcome those who are pushed aside or treated unfairly by society. God the Holy Spirit, our Helper, gives us the courage to accept this responsibility to welcome and care for all, as Jesus did.

The Church Heals and Forgives

The Holy Spirit helped the disciples to carry on Jesus' mission of healing and forgiving. The New Testament has many stories about the disciples healing and caring for people's bodies, encouraging people to turn away from sin and be forgiven by God. They brought God's forgiveness and peace to all in Jesus' name.

The Church Serves

The first Christians never forgot that Jesus "did not come to be served, but to serve" (Matthew 20:28). They also remembered His commandment, "As I have loved you, so you must love one another" (John 13:34).

Jesus' disciples took special care of people in need, such as widows, orphans, and the poor. They knew that every baptized Christian was to take part in this work of justice and mercy.

The **ascension** is the event in which Jesus Christ was taken into heaven after the resurrection.

The Body of Christ

Today the Church carries on the mission that Jesus gave to His first disciples to heal and forgive. When the Church, by the power of the Holy Spirit, brings healing and forgiveness to one person in the name of Jesus, the whole Church shares in that joy.

Saint Paul said that we are all connected like the parts of a body. "If one part of the body suffers, the other parts suffer with it; if one part is praised, all the other parts share its happiness" (1 Corinthians 12:26). Jesus is the head of His body, the Church, and we are its members.

The Church continues to serve all people. Like Jesus, each member of the Church can give something to others. For example, we can give a special talent, a piece of clothing, or some food. The best gift we can give is the gift of ourselves and our time.

By Baptism we become members of Christ's body, the Church. As we work together, everyone's gifts are important. This means that each of us is a very important member of the body of Christ. Everyone has a part to play in carrying on the mission of Jesus. We must work together in this great mission.

33

COMING TO FAITH

Describe the ways in which the early Church carried on Jesus' mission.

Talk together about your parish. How does it:

- welcome?
- heal?
- forgive?
- serve?
- act justly?
- bring peace?

Choose one of the above. What can fifth graders do to help out?

PRACTICING FAITH

Talk over these ideas about ways to serve your parish:

- welcome the newly baptized.
- form a "cleanup" group for the church and grounds.
- distribute or sort food and clothing for parish outreach.
- write a letter to a local newspaper about an issue of justice and peace.
- serve as ushers, gift bearers, or choir members at a parish liturgy.
- Other: _____

After you decide what your group will do, ask yourselves questions like these:

- Whom should we talk to in our parish?
- What adults do we need to help us?
- When will we do this service?

† Form a prayer circle. After a moment of quiet, pray together:

Jesus, we come to You with all our gifts and with our faults, too. We want to follow You as Your disciples. Help us as we place ourselves at the service of others in Your name. Amen.

Talk with your catechist about ways you and your family might use the "Faith Alive" pages together. Encourage a family member to become involved, if possible, in your service project and choose a time to pray the prayer together.

FAITH ALIVE AT HOME AND IN THE PARISH

Your fifth grader has learned more about the way our Church began and how it continues Jesus' mission of welcoming, healing, forgiving, and serving today. A central theme of the Second Vatican Council is that, by Baptism, all of us are called to share in the mission and ministry of the Church—each according to his or her gifts.

You might ask yourself:

■ *How do I help to carry on the mission of Jesus Christ?*

If possible, read the first chapter of the Acts of the Apostles. Then choose a family project for all to work on together and to share their gifts as the early Christians did.

Help the Church come alive for your family. Ask your fifth grader to tell the story of how the Church began at Pentecost. Then have him or her do the following activity.

† Family Prayer

Pray this prayer that God may heal the sickness or poor health of a family member, or any separation caused by an argument.

Jesus Christ, our Savior and Messiah, send the Holy Spirit to help us bring forgiveness and healing to the people in our lives who need it. By doing this, may Your body, the Church, grow and carry on Your mission in the world. Amen.

Learn by heart Faith Summary

● The Holy Spirit helps the Church carry on the mission of Jesus to all people.

● Jesus is the head of the Church, His body, and we are its members.

● Like Jesus, the Church serves people and brings them Jesus' healing and forgiveness.

Reporting the Pentecost Event

You are a reporter present at the first Pentecost. Write a headline for your eyewitness account for the *Jerusalem Journal*. Act out what happened.

Jerusalem Journal

Review

Before doing this *Review*, have your fifth grader go over the *Faith Summary*. Encourage your child to learn the three points by heart. The answers to numbers 1–4 appear on page 216. The response to number 5 will show how much your fifth grader wants to be involved in the mission of the Church. When the *Review* is completed, go over it together.

Circle the letter beside the correct answer.

1. The disciples received the Holy Spirit on
   a. Easter.
   b. Passover.
   c. Pentecost.
   d. Christmas.

2. Saint Paul compared the Church to
   a. a company.
   b. the body of Christ.
   c. a mustard seed.
   d. a storm at sea.

3. The Church is to serve
   a. some people.
   b. all people.
   c. only Catholics.
   d. only grown-ups.

4. Today the mission of the Church is to
   a. welcome all people.
   b. forgive and heal people.
   c. serve people.
   d. all of the above

5. How will you be part of the Church that welcomes, forgives, heals, and serves?

   _____

   _____

   _____

FAMILY SCRIPTURE MOMENT

Gather and invite family members to look at a picture of or draw a healthy tree or plant. Ask: What would happen to the branches if we cut them off? What would happen if we fed, watered and cared for the tree or plant? Then **Listen** as Jesus uses the image of the vine and the branches.

"I am the vine, and you are the branches. Whoever remains in Me, and I in that person, will bear much fruit; for you can do nothing without Me. Whoever does not remain in Me is thrown out like a branch and dries up. If you remain in Me and My words remain in you, then you will ask for anything you wish, and you shall have it. My Father's glory is shown by your bearing much fruit; and in this way you become My disciples."

From John 15:5–8

Share what each one heard in this reading.

Consider for family enrichment:

■ Jesus uses the familiar image of the grapevine to express His unity with His disciples. The very life of Jesus is in us, just as the life of the vine is in each connected leaf.

■ We receive the very life of Jesus through the sacraments and remain in Him by our prayer and service to others.

Reflect and **Decide** What good fruit might Jesus be calling us to produce? Link arms and pray: Jesus, keep us joined to You and to one another!

5 The Sacraments and the Church

OUR LIFE

Kate loves her grandmother. They talk to each other on the phone several times a week. Kate feels that she can tell her grandmother everything and her grandmother really listens! She doesn't criticize, but she gives Kate good advice. Kate loves the way her grandmother talks to her. "She treats me like a person," Kate says.

How do Kate and her grandmother show each other love and respect?

How do you show respect to others?

Darryl was upset after soccer practice. "Coach Tate just doesn't like me," he complained to his friend Sam. "You're crazy," Sam replied. "Whatever made you come up with that idea? Has he told you that?"

"It's not what he says; it's how he acts," said Darryl. "He never puts me in the game. And he turns away when I come near him."

What signs made Darryl think the coach didn't like him?

Explain how actions can sometimes "speak louder than words."

What signs do you give people to let them know how you feel about them?

SHARING LIFE

People give us many signs of caring or not caring about us. Discuss together what some of these signs might be.

Imagine some of the signs that Jesus wants us to give to other people.

Signs of God's Love

Signs of God's love are everywhere for us to see if we are willing to notice them. A *sign* is something visible that tells us about something invisible.

Jesus used many signs to show God's love. For example, He reminded farmers that they looked at signs in nature to predict the weather. He said,

Salvador Dali, *The Last Supper,* 1955

"When you see a cloud in the west, you say that it is going to rain—and it does. And when you feel the south wind blowing, you say that it is going to get hot—and it does."

Jesus said we should look for signs of God's love just as we look for signs of the weather.
From Luke 12:54–56

We find the greatest signs of God's love in Jesus' words and actions. Jesus is the perfect sign of God to us. Saint Paul called Jesus "the visible likeness of the invisible God" (Colossians 1:15). Paul meant that in Jesus we meet the Son of God made flesh.

The Son of God became one of us and shared our everyday lives. Because Jesus is God, He is the perfect sign of God's love for all humankind. In Jesus we meet God's very Self. This is why we say that Jesus is the Sacrament of God to us.

A sacrament is the most effective kind of sign. It causes to happen the very thing for which it stands. Jesus is the greatest Sacrament of God because He is God with us.

Our Church is also a sign, or sacrament, of Jesus for us. We meet Jesus each time our Church welcomes, forgives, teaches, serves, and works for justice and peace.

But our Church is not always a perfect sign of Jesus Christ because it is made up of many imperfect people, including ourselves. As each of us becomes a better sign, the whole body of Christ, the Church, becomes a more effective sign, or sacrament, of Jesus.

Seven Special Signs

The seven sacraments—Baptism, Confirmation, Eucharist, Reconciliation, Anointing of the Sick, Matrimony, and Holy Orders—are effective signs of Jesus' presence with us.

These seven sacraments are called effective signs because they do more than ordinary signs. Through the power of the Holy Spirit,

A **sacrament** is an effective sign through which Jesus Christ shares God's life and love with us.

THE SEVEN SACRAMENTS

Baptism, Confirmation, and Eucharist

The Church carries on Jesus' mission of welcoming members into the body of Christ when we celebrate Baptism, Confirmation, and Eucharist. We call these the sacraments of initiation.

Reconciliation and Anointing of the Sick

The Church forgives and heals as Jesus did by celebrating Reconciliation and Anointing of the Sick. We call these the sacraments of healing.

Matrimony and Holy Orders

The Church serves others and is a special sign of God's love by celebrating and living the sacraments of Matrimony and Holy Orders. We call these the sacraments of service.

they actually bring about what they promise. The sacraments are the most effective signs of Jesus' presence with us.

In the sacraments, Jesus shares God's life with the Church by the power of the Holy Spirit. He calls us to respond by living as His disciples. In the seven sacraments, Jesus Christ, the Son of God, really and truly comes to us in our lives today.

God's life and love in us is called grace. *Grace* is a sharing in the divine life, in God's very life and love. We receive God's grace in the sacraments.

By celebrating the sacraments, the Church worships and praises God. In celebrating the sacraments, the Church becomes a powerful sign of Jesus' presence and God's reign in our world.

Coming To Faith

How is Jesus a sign, or sacrament, of God's love for you?

How can you be a sign of God's love to others today?

Practicing Faith

Form seven small groups, one for each sacrament. As your group is named, step forward. At the end the groups should be in a single circle.

Leader: Baptism! (Group 1 steps forward.)

Group 1: We thank You, O God, for the gift of new life with which you have blessed us.

Leader: Confirmation!

Group 2: We bless You, O God, for the Holy Spirit, who strengthens us for service in Your Church and in the world.

Leader: Eucharist!

Group 3: Our lives are nourished with the Body and Blood of Christ.

Leader: Reconciliation!

Group 4: Blessed are we, O God, with Your forgiveness and mercy and peace.

Leader: Anointing of the Sick!

Group 5: You bless us, O God, with this healing sacrament. You comfort, console, and give us peace.

Leader: Holy Orders!

Group 6: Continue to bless Your Church, O God, with the gift of this sacrament of ministry and service.

Leader: Matrimony!

Group 7: Thank You, O God, for this sacrament that blesses our lives with married love and families.

All: (stretching hands out to center of circle, palms down) For all these signs of Your love and grace that bless our lives, thank You, God! Amen.

40

Talk with your catechist about ways you and your family might use the "Faith Alive" pages. You might want to use the blessing prayer at a meal during the week.

FAITH ALIVE AT HOME AND IN THE PARISH

Your fifth grader has been introduced in a deeper way to the seven sacraments. She or he has been taught that Jesus is the perfect sign, or sacrament, of God and that the Church is the sacrament of Jesus. Each of us, as a member of the Church, is called to carry on Jesus' mission of welcoming, healing, forgiving, and serving. Here are some things your family can do to be signs of Jesus. Take some extra time to listen to your daughter or son. Share with each other the events of the day. Encourage surprise hugs among all family members. Say "I'm sorry" if you hurt one another. Encourage your fifth grader to do the activity below.

† Family Prayer

Leader: We thank You, O God, for the blessings of our lives.

All: For being welcomed into the Church, the body of Christ, at Baptism.
For being more closely united with one another through the Eucharist.
For being forgiven when we sin.

Leader: For all of these blessings we thank You, O God.

Signs of God's Love

Write on pieces of paper ways your family can be signs of God's love. Each day select one and read it aloud. Encourage one another to practice it. Write some of your ideas on cards, and make a wreath as shown below.

Learn by heart Faith Summary

- A sacrament is an effective sign through which Jesus Christ shares God's life and love with us.

- There are seven sacraments: Baptism, Confirmation, Eucharist, Reconciliation, Anointing of the Sick, Matrimony, and Holy Orders.

- We receive God's grace in the sacraments.

CALL GRANDMA

CLEAN ROOM

PRAY FOR OTHERS

Review

Before doing this *Review*, have your fifth grader go over the *Faith Summary*. Encourage your child to learn the first and second statements by heart. The answers to numbers 1–4 appear on page 216. The response to number 5 will help you see how well your fifth grader is trying to be a sign of God's love. When the *Review* is completed, go over it together.

Circle the letter beside the correct answer.

1. Jesus is a sign of
   a. a pain-free future.
   b. God's love.
   c. fear.
   d. hopelessness.

2. The sacraments of initiation are
   a. Confirmation and Matrimony.
   b. Anointing, Eucharist, Baptism.
   c. Baptism, Confirmation, Eucharist.
   d. Reconciliation, Baptism, Eucharist.

3. The Church
   a. gives us the sacraments.
   b. carries on the mission of Jesus.
   c. works for God's reign.
   d. all of the above

4. God's life and love in us is called
   a. original sin.
   b. grace.
   c. sins.
   d. worship.

5. How will you be a sign of God's love to others this week?

_____

_____

_____

_____

FAMILY SCRIPTURE MOMENT

Gather and ask: What are some of the non-material things in life that we thirst for? Then **Listen** as Jesus leads us to find living water.

On the last day of the feast of Tabernacles Jesus stood up and said in a loud voice, "Whoever is thirsty should come to Me and drink. As the Scripture says, 'Whoever believes in Me, streams of life-giving water will pour from that person's heart." Jesus said this about the Spirit that those who believed in Him were going to receive. At that time the Spirit had not yet been given, because Jesus had not been raised to glory.
From John 7:37–39

Share what thirst in your life Jesus can satisfy and why.

Consider for family enrichment:

■ Jesus uses the Old Testament image of life-giving waters to prepare His disciples for the coming of the Holy Spirit after the resurrection.

■ Through the sacramental life of the Church, we can constantly drink the living water of the Holy Spirit.

Reflect and **Decide** What are the spiritual gifts for which we thirst, those that might transform us, our Church, and our world? How will we as a family bring our "thirst" and needs to Jesus?

6 | Celebrating Reconciliation

OUR LIFE

In eastern Africa there is a fascinating tribe called the Masai. They are very tall, beautiful people who live gently and calmly in harmony with themselves and the natural world around them. This harmony is so important to the Masai that if one family offends another the whole tribe is upset. The whole tribe works to bring the separated families together so there can be peace and reconciliation.

The tribe members encourage the two families to prepare special foods, which they then bring to the center of the village. Everyone encourages them and cheers them on. The two families then exchange their food with each other and sit down to eat. This is the sign of forgiveness. The whole tribe then celebrates the return of peace and harmony.

What do you think about the Masai sign of forgiveness?

How do you show signs of forgiveness?

SHARING LIFE

What can we learn from the Masai for our lives?

Talk together about the best ways to show forgiveness in our culture.

Good News of Forgiveness

God sent Jesus to show us that God is always waiting to forgive our sins, no matter how bad they are. Jesus taught us that God always forgives us when we are sorry for our sins and ask God's forgiveness.

Jesus understood that living as His disciples and doing God's loving will are not always easy. He knew that His followers might sin and need God's forgiveness.

Here is a gospel story in which Jesus tells the disciples to forgive sins in His name.

Late the first Easter Sunday evening, Jesus' disciples were hiding in a locked room. They were afraid that the people who crucified Jesus would kill them, too.

Jesus came and said, "Peace be with you."

After looking at the wounds in Jesus' hands and side, they were amazed and filled with joy. They knew it was Jesus.

Jesus said to them again, "Peace be with you. As the Father sent me, I now send you. If you forgive people's sins, they are forgiven."

From John 20:19–23

Our Church Forgives

Today our Church continues Jesus' mission of forgiveness in the sacrament of Reconciliation. We prepare ourselves to celebrate Reconciliation by examining our conscience and by becoming aware of our sins.

We think about our sins or the things that showed we did not follow the way of Jesus. We are sorry for what we have done that is wrong. We remember that God is always ready to forgive us if we are sorry. We can think about the story of the prodigal son and his forgiving father (Luke 15:11–24).

When we examine our conscience, we may ask ourselves questions like these:

● Do I show that I love God?

● Does God come first in my life, or are other things more important to me?

● Have I used God's name with respect, or have I sometimes said God's name in anger?

● Do I take part in Mass on Sundays and on holy days of obligation, or have I missed Mass for no serious reason?

● Do I obey my parents or guardians or have I disobeyed them?

● Do I show that I love other people as I love myself?

44

● Have I tried to act lovingly to others, or have I hurt anyone by my words or deeds?

● Have I shared my things with others, or have I been selfish or taken others' things without permission?

● Have I been truthful and fair, or have I lied and cheated?

● Have I cared about the poor, the hungry, and those who are oppressed?

● Do I try to be a peacemaker and treat everyone with justice?

● Do I try to live like Jesus?

After we have examined our conscience and are sorry for our sins, we are ready to continue with the celebration of the sacrament of Reconciliation.

COMING TO FAITH

Take a minute to look again at the examination of conscience. Then work in groups or with a partner to change each question into several "we can..." statements. For example:

Do I show that I love God? We can show we love God by being more patient with those who annoy us.

Share all your "we can..." statements with your group.

PRACTICING FAITH

A Prayer Service of Forgiveness

Opening Hymn

Theme

We praise and thank God for God's love and forgiveness.

Greeting

Leader: Jesus brings us God's forgiveness. May the peace and mercy of Jesus be with you.

All: And also with you.

Leader: Jesus, we have come to celebrate God's forgiveness. Hear us as we ask for Your forgiveness and peace.

All: Amen.

First Reading

God is always ready to forgive us. A reading from the Book of Joel. (Read Joel 2:13.)

Responsorial Psalm

Leader: Teach me, O God, what You want me to do, and I will obey You faithfully.

All: Great is Your love for us, O God.

Leader: You, O God, are a merciful and loving God, always patient, always kind, and always faithful. Turn to me and have mercy on me.

All: Great is Your love for us, O God.

Gospel

The group may act out the gospel story about the prodigal son (Luke 15:11–24) or several readers may take different parts and read it together.

Examination of Conscience

A member of the group reads the examination of conscience questions on page 45. After each question is read, pause for quiet reflection. Then pray:

Leader: Jesus, forgive us our sins.

All: Lord, hear our prayer.

Leader: Jesus, help us to love one another.

All: Lord, have mercy on us.

Leader: Jesus, give us the courage to turn away from sin and to change our lives.

All: Lord, forgive us our sins.

Leader: Jesus, free us from our sins and lead us to the freedom enjoyed by Your faithful disciples.

All: (Pray the Our Father together.)

A Prayer of Praise

Select a psalm as a prayer of praise, for example, Psalm 136:1–9 or Psalm 145:1–13.

Sign of Peace

Share with one another a greeting of peace.

Closing Hymn

FAITH ALIVE AT HOME AND IN THE PARISH

This liturgical lesson provided your fifth grader with a further development of the meaning and grace of the sacrament of Reconciliation and a deepened awareness of the meaning of forgiveness. The ability and desire to forgive others and to ask forgiveness of others is one of the greatest virtues we can develop in our children. Forgiveness is a mature virtue, but it can be modeled and encouraged from your child's earliest years. When children witness and experience forgiveness in their homes, they more readily practice it themselves.

The first Christians, learning from their Hebrew roots in the Old Testament, came to realize that sins committed after Baptism are an offense to the whole community—that sin cuts us off from God's people. When they faced the problem of being reconciled for those sins, they might have remembered the Israelite Day of Atonement, on which the *whole people* approached God *as a people* to seek mercy. They surely remembered the parables and the example and words of Jesus and His ministry of forgiving sinners.

The sacrament of Reconciliation emphasizes the role of the Church community in our celebration of this sacrament. Since our sins are against one another and take from the holiness of the community, it is most fitting that our sacramental reconciliation with God should be through the ministry of the Church.

† Family Prayer: Forgiveness

Jesus, we come to celebrate Your forgiveness. We do this by forgiving one another. Give us open hearts. Through Your gift of forgiveness, bring our family harmony and peace. Help us to be Your peacemakers in our world. Amen.

Learn by heart Faith Summary

- God is always ready to forgive our sins.
- Jesus gave His disciples the power to forgive sins.
- Reconciliation is the sacrament in which we are forgiven by God through the ministry of the Church.

Share with your family how the Masai restored peace and harmony through a forgiveness rite. Talk about ways your family can share forgiveness. Describe these ideas below.

_____

_____

_____

_____

_____

47

Review

Go over the *Faith Summary* together and encourage your fifth grader to learn it by heart, especially the third statement. Then complete the *Review*. The answers to numbers 1–4 appear on page 216. The response to number 5 will indicate how well your son or daughter understands the rite of Reconciliation.

Fill in the circle next to the correct answer.

1. Jesus gave the apostles power to
  ○ forgive sins in His name.
  ○ walk on water.
  ○ ascend into heaven.

2. Jesus' mission of forgiveness continues in
  ○ the Our Father.
  ○ the sacrament of Reconciliation
  ○ the sacrament of Holy Orders.

3. Jesus always forgives us
  ○ when we are sorry.
  ○ even when we are not sorry.
  ○ whether we need it or not.

4. We prepare for Reconciliation by
  ○ fasting for one hour.
  ○ using holy water.
  ○ making an examination of conscience.

5. Tell what happens when you celebrate the sacrament of Reconciliation.

_____

_____

_____

_____

FAMILY SCRIPTURE MOMENT

Gather and ask: How do we feel when others accuse or blame us? Then **Listen** to this story of Jesus forgiving the woman caught in adultery.

"Teacher," her accusers said to Jesus, "this woman was caught committing adultery. Moses commanded that such a woman must be stoned to death. Now, what do you say?" They said this to trap Jesus. He said to them, "Whichever one of you has committed no sin may throw the first stone." When they heard this, they all left, one by one. Jesus said to the woman, "Is there no one left to condemn you?" "No one, sir," she answered. "Well, then," Jesus said, "I do not condemn you either. Go, but do not sin again."
From John 8:4–7, 9–11

Share what you learn for your own life from this Scripture story.

Consider for family enrichment:

■ By refusing to condemn the woman, Jesus teaches His disciples to be merciful as God is merciful.

■ As disciples of Jesus we are called to grow rich in mercy, compassion, and understanding.

Reflect and **Decide** What are some of the ways we can help one another to avoid sin? Pray together: Lord Jesus, let us be peacemakers. Help us to recognize our own sins, rather than pointing a finger at others.

7 Celebrating Eucharist

Jesus, help us
who share the
Bread of Life
to become one
in mind and
heart.

Our Life

In the Old Testament we read about a man named Elisha, who lived long ago. Elisha helped those who were sick or poor.

One time a woman explained to him that her husband had just died and that a man to whom her husband owed money had come to her demanding to be paid. The woman was very poor, and her family no longer even had food to eat. All that was left in her home was a small jar of olive oil.

Elisha instructed her to go home and borrow as many empty jars as she could. He told her to start pouring the olive oil from the small jar that she had into all the other jars her sons could bring to her.

Elisha smiled when the woman returned and told him that she had a house filled with jars of olive oil. He said to her, "Sell the olive oil and pay all your debts. There will be enough money left over for your family to live on."
From 2 Kings 4:1–7

What did you learn from this story?

Who gives you what you need for life?

Sharing Life

Imagine you could ask Elisha for a certain food or drink that would never run out. What would you ask for? Why?

Did Jesus give us any special food?

What is it? How does it help us?

Food That Lasts Forever

The early Christians frequently shared the special meal Jesus gave us. They followed the instruction that Jesus gave to His disciples at the Last Supper, "Do this in memory of me" (1 Corinthians 11:24).

They came together to celebrate the Eucharist. They sang songs; remembered Jesus' teachings; and recalled His life, death, and resurrection. They took bread and wine and did what Jesus did at the Last Supper. Then they shared in the Body and Blood of Christ together.

Jesus Himself is the Bread of Life, the food that we receive in the Eucharist. Jesus is really present with us in the Eucharist to nourish and strengthen us to live for the reign of God.

One time Jesus told the people, "I am the Bread of Life. Whoever comes to Me will never be hungry; whoever believes in Me will never be thirsty" (from John 6:35).

One with Jesus and Others

Celebrating the Eucharist together as the Church is the most powerful sign of our unity with Jesus Christ and with one another.

Teaching about the Eucharist as a sign of our unity with Jesus and one another, Saint Paul wrote:

"When we drink from the cup we use in the Lord's Supper, we are sharing in the Blood of Christ. When we eat the Bread we break, we are sharing in the Body of Christ. All of us, though many, are one, for we all share the same Bread."

From 1 Corinthians 10:16–17

We come together as the community of Jesus' followers to share in His life and love. In our eucharistic assembly, we unite ourselves with Jesus and the Church all over the world. We are the sign of Jesus' life and love in the world.

Our Thanksgiving Prayer

The Eucharist is both a meal and a sacrifice. At Mass we celebrate the Eucharist. It is the Christian community's greatest prayer of praise and thanksgiving to God.

In the *Introductory Rites* we prepare for our celebration. We remember that we are the community of Jesus' disciples.

The Scripture readings in the *Liturgy of the Word* recall how we are to live as the people of God, the body of Christ. We listen carefully, because God speaks to us through the Scripture readings. We learn how to live for the reign of God, as Jesus taught.

In the *Liturgy of the Eucharist* we praise and thank God for Jesus, God's own Son. Jesus gave Himself for us. We give thanks that through Jesus we are made one again with God and one another.

The priest breaks the Bread because we who are many are one in the sharing of the one Bread. We receive the gift of Jesus, our Bread of Life, in Holy Communion. We give thanks to Jesus for coming to us.

We pray and receive God's blessing in the *Concluding Rite*. We go forth and try to show our family, our neighbors, and even strangers that we are the body of Christ in the world today. We try to live as disciples of Jesus.

Coming To Faith

What food do we receive in the sacrament of the Eucharist?

_____

_____

Why is the Mass the most important sign of our unity with Jesus and the Church?

_____

_____

_____

How will you show that you are thankful for the gift of Jesus in Holy Communion?

_____

_____

_____

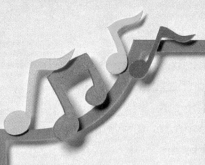

PRACTICING FAITH

Planning a Celebration of the Eucharist
Plan your Mass celebration together in small groups.

Theme: Look at the readings for the Mass of the day. Read the Opening Prayer. What is the prayer about? Write it here.

_____

_____

_____

_____

Hymn: Choose an opening hymn for your Mass. Write the title here.

_____

Readings: Name the readings for the Mass of the day. You can find these readings in a book called the Lectionary. List the readings and who will read them.

_____

_____

_____

_____

Prayer of the Faithful: Write several petitions that express your thanks and the thanksgiving of your group to God. Write them here.

_____

_____

_____

_____

Presentation of the Gifts: Decide who will present the gifts of bread and wine and write their names here.

Gift	Presenter
_____	_____
_____	_____

Hymn: Choose a closing hymn. Write the title here.

_____

_____

Share your ideas with the whole group and create a single plan.

FAITH ALIVE AT HOME AND IN THE PARISH

In this liturgical lesson the fifth graders are drawn into a deeper understanding of the Eucharist by planning a celebration of the Mass.

For Catholic Christians, the Eucharist is the spiritual meal in which we are fed by the Lord with His Body and Blood. During the celebration, we hear the word of God proclaimed in the readings. We respond with words of thanksgiving and praise. We are invited to share in the communal meal by the priest who presides at our sacrifice of praise.

In the Eucharist we become one with Jesus because we do this eucharistic action in memory of Him. Being fed at the Lord's table means we have been nourished anew for the journey. We in turn need to feed others, share with others, and serve others in Jesus' name. Our Eucharist is our feast in order that we can fast with those who hunger and thirst after justice.

Your family might want to "go in peace" from the Eucharist to reach out to those who are physically hungry at a local shelter or soup kitchen. Or perhaps you might prepare a dinner for a neighbor who is disabled or housebound.

† Family Prayer

Jesus, You are the Bread of Life. If we come to You, we will never be hungry. If we believe in You, we will never be thirsty. Help us to respond to all the hungers and thirsts that we find in those we meet.

Make a prayer card for your table. Start a family custom: whenever you gather for a family meal a family member prays this prayer as a reminder of the unseen Guest among you.

Learn by heart Faith Summary

● At Mass we celebrate the Eucharist, our greatest prayer of thanksgiving and praise.

● In the Liturgy of the Word we listen as God speaks to us in the readings.

● In the Liturgy of the Eucharist we praise and thank God through Jesus, whom we receive in Holy Communion.

Christ, invisible Guest at all our meals, come and be with us.

Review

Go over the *Faith Summary* with your fifth grader. Encourage him or her to learn it by heart. Then complete the *Review*. The answers to numbers 1–4 appear on page 216. The response to number 5 will help to indicate your fifth grader's understanding of the Eucharist. When the *Review* is completed, go over it together.

Circle the letter next to the correct answer.

1. Jesus said that whoever comes to Him will
   a. sit at His right side.
   b. rule the world.
   c. never be hungry.

2. Paul said that all of us who share the Body of Christ
   a. are one.
   b. are teachers.
   c. are apostles.

3. In the Eucharist we come together as Jesus' followers to
   a. share in the life and love of Jesus.
   b. unite ourselves with Jesus and the Church.
   c. both a and b

4. Circle the letter to show what does not belong to the Mass.
   a. Liturgy of the Word
   b. stations of the cross
   c. Liturgy of the Eucharist

5. Jesus said, "I am the Bread of Life." Explain what this means for your life.

_____

_____

_____

 **FAMILY SCRIPTURE MOMENT**

Gather and recall improvised meals for friends when there were more guests than expected. Ask: Why and how do we feed people when there may not be "enough food to go around"? Then **Listen** to the story of Jesus feeding a hungry crowd.

"Make the people sit down," Jesus told His disciples. So all the people sat down; there were about five thousand in all. Jesus took the bread, gave thanks to God, and distributed it to the people. He did the same with the fish, and they all had as much as they wanted. When they were all full, Jesus said to His disciples, "Gather the pieces left over." So they gathered them all and filled twelve baskets with the pieces left over from the five barley loaves which the people had eaten.

From John 6:10–13

Share what you hear this gospel story saying for your life.

Consider for family enrichment:

■ By feeding the crowd with a few loaves and fishes, Jesus shows His concern for all who are hungry and gives a sign that He is the Bread of Life for all.

■ In the celebration of the Eucharist, we become signs of Jesus' love for a hungry world.

Reflect and **Decide** How might our parish feed those who hunger for bread? for the Bible? for dignity and self-esteem?

UNIT 1 ▪ REVIEW

Jesus Christ Reveals God

Jesus Christ is truly human. Jesus was like us in every way except that He never sinned. Jesus Christ is also truly divine. Jesus is God's own Son. Jesus revealed by His words and deeds that "God is love" (1 John 4:8). Today, God works through us and other people to show God's love in the world.

Jesus Christ and the Kingdom of God

Jesus showed by His words and actions that He was the Messiah. Jesus announced the good news of the kingdom, or reign, of God. The good news is that God loves us and will always be with us.

Jesus brought about the reign of God by His words and actions. Jesus showed us how to live for the reign of God by loving God, our neighbor, and ourselves.

Jesus Christ Blesses Our Lives

Jesus Christ invited everyone to live for the reign of God. Jesus forgave people their sins. By His words and actions Jesus lived His whole life helping and serving others. We live for the reign of God by following the example of Jesus.

The Church Carries on Jesus' Mission

After Jesus' ascension into heaven, the Holy Spirit came to Jesus' disciples and filled them with gifts to preach the good news to everyone. The Holy Spirit continues to help our Church to carry on the mission of Jesus to all people.

The Church welcomes all people to believe in Jesus and to follow Him. The Church forgives and heals, as Jesus did. Every member of the Church is called to carry on Jesus' mission by serving others.

The Sacraments and the Church

There are many signs of God's love in our everyday life. The Church is the sacrament of Jesus. The most effective signs of God's presence in our Church are the seven sacraments.

Baptism, Confirmation, and Eucharist are called sacraments of initiation. Through these sacraments the Church welcomes all people into the community of the Church.

Reconciliation and the Anointing of the Sick are sacraments of healing. Through these sacraments the Church brings us God's forgiveness when we sin, and strengthens us when we are sick.

Matrimony and Holy Orders are sacraments of service. Through these sacraments the Church continues Jesus' mission of service through married couples and through our ordained ministers: bishops, priests, and deacons.

UNIT 1 · TEST

Circle the answers.

1. Jesus was
   a. human.
   b. divine.
   c. both human and divine.
   d. an angel sent by God.

2. Jesus revealed to us that
   a. God cares about us.
   b. God is love.
   c. God forgives us.
   d. all of these

3. Jesus began His work by
   a. ascending into heaven.
   b. announcing the reign of God.
   c. dying on the cross.
   d. sending the Holy Spirit.

4. Jesus forgave sins to show that
   a. He was reconciling us with God.
   b. God forgives only some people.
   c. God only forgives some of our sins.
   d. we do not need to forgive others.

5. The most powerful signs of Jesus' presence in the Church are
   a. parish churches.
   b. priests.
   c. the seven sacraments.
   d. parents.

Complete the following statements.

6. Baptism, Confirmation, and Eucharist are called sacraments of initiation because

_____

_____

7. Reconciliation and Anointing of the sick are called sacraments of healing because

_____

_____

8. Matrimony and Holy Orders are called sacraments of service because

_____

_____

Think and decide:

9. To me the reign of God means

_____

_____

10. I will show that I live for God's reign by

_____

_____

Name _____

Your son or daughter has just completed Unit 1. Have him or her bring this paper to the catechist. It will help you and the catechist know better how to help your fifth grader grow in faith.

_____ He or she needs help with the part of the Review I have underlined.

_____ He or she understands what has been taught in this unit.

_____ I would like to speak with you. My phone number is _____ .

Signature: _____

8 Jesus Christ Brings Us Life
(Baptism)

Come, Holy
Spirit, help us
be signs of
Your life to
others.

OUR LIFE

Finish the story.

Angie went out on the tractor with her father
as he plowed the field. She breathed in
the wonderful smell of the earth as it was
turned over to receive the new seed. In the
spring days that followed, the gentle rains
and warm sunshine made it a perfect
growing season. Then one morning Angie
saw the first green shoots of wheat covering
the field. She ran out into the fields.
Stooping down, she touched the new wheat
shoots and whispered,

"_____"

What does life mean to you?

Each of us has dreams about our life. What
are some of your dreams about life for
yourself? for others? for our world?

SHARING LIFE

Discuss together.

Give some reasons why you believe that
life is God's greatest gift to us.

What do you imagine God wants us to do
with the gift of life?

Come up with some good reasons why you
think water is used as a sign of new life in the
sacrament of Baptism.

Baptism, A Sacrament of Initiation

When we are born, we become members of families. Then there is another important family that we are invited to join—the Church. By Baptism we join, or begin our initiation into, the Church, the body of Christ. We are freed from the power of original sin and become children of God.

By Baptism we are united with Jesus in His death and resurrection. We die to sin and rise to new life as Jesus did. Baptism enables us to live as God's own people with new life for doing God's loving will.

Many parishes celebrate Baptism during a Sunday Mass. This reminds all present of their own Baptism and of their responsibility to help new members to live their faith.

During the celebration of Baptism a priest or deacon blesses the water that will be used as a sign of rebirth. The celebrant prays, "We ask you, Father, with your Son to send the Holy Spirit upon the water of this font. May all who are buried with Christ in the death of baptism rise also with him to newness of life."

The priest or deacon pours the water on the heads of the people being baptized, or immerses them, saying, "(*Name*), I baptize you in the name of the Father, and of the Son, and of the Holy Spirit." The water and these words are the signs of the sacrament of Baptism.

At this moment they are reborn of water and the Holy Spirit. They receive new life. They are reborn into the divine life of God's grace, become members of the Church, the body of Christ, and receive the responsibility to live for God's reign.

The newly baptized are next anointed with holy oil, as Christ was anointed priest, prophet, and king. This shows that they share in Jesus' work of bringing about God's justice and peace.

The newly baptized are also given a white garment and a candle. The white garment shows that they have put on the new life of the risen Christ. A candle, lit from the Easter candle, is held. This is a sign that the baptized are to keep the light of Christ burning brightly by following Jesus Christ always.

Living Our Baptism

Most of us were probably very young when we were baptized. At that time our parents and godparents promised to help us live our new life as Christians. When we are old enough, we must also make this choice and renew our baptismal promises for ourselves.

58

No one can live our Baptism for us. We receive God's grace and the support of others. We have the Holy Spirit to help us live our new life as disciples of Jesus. Our parents, friends, and the whole Christian community give us support. But we must choose now to live the way of Jesus.

Here are some signs that show you are trying to keep your baptismal promises:

● On waking, you thank God for another day and ask God to help you live the new life of Baptism.

● You decide who in your family needs a laugh, a hug, or a little help. You give it.

● You try to help those in need and to be a peacemaker between angry friends.

● You cooperate with your catechist so that you learn and grow in living your Catholic faith.

● On your way to and from school and on weekends, you see whether there are people in your neighborhood you can help.

● In your family or parish, you help teach younger children their prayers.

● You celebrate the sacrament of Reconciliation regularly. You listen carefully as the priest advises you how to live each day well.

● With your family, you take part in Mass on Sunday or Saturday evening. If they do not go, you try to go to Mass with others and ask God to help and bless your family.

● Each night you thank God for the day. You ask God to help you to become a peacemaker and to be fair and loving to all.

Priest, Prophet, King

Jesus was a priest, a prophet, and a king. He was a priest by offering His life to God, a prophet by calling us to do God's loving will, and a king by showing us how to let God reign in our lives.

COMING TO FAITH

Work together to create a collage or a mural of the signs of Baptism. Call it "Signs of New Life." Illustrate with drawings or pictures of water, a candle, a white garment, and holy oil. Then explain briefly what each signifies.

PRACTICING FAITH

Talk together about ways your group might be of service to people in your parish preparing for Baptism. If possible, invite your pastor to discuss with you ways you might contribute.

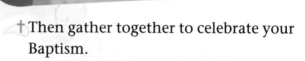

† Then gather together to celebrate your Baptism.

Leader: Through Baptism we have become your beloved sons and daughters.

All: Blessed be God.

Leader: We have been born again of water and the Holy Spirit.

All: Blessed be God.

Leader: Help us to be faithful disciples of Jesus Christ and His witnesses.

All: Blessed be God.

End your prayer by making the sign of the cross together.

Talk with your catechist about ways you and your family might use the "Faith Alive" pages together. Invite your family to talk about ways of being signs of new life to others this week. Close this lesson by praying the baptismal blessing with your catechist and friends.

To help your fifth grader to appreciate better the sacrament of Baptism talked about in this lesson, tell the story of her or his own Baptism. Talk about what it means to live one's baptismal promises. By our Baptism we are called to holiness of life and active participation in the mission of the Church. Share how sacramental celebration should be a time of joy and celebration for the whole parish family.

You can make use of the many opportunities that arise to deepen the Christian life begun at Baptism. Each celebration of the Eucharist and of Reconciliation brings us into contact with the mystery of Christ's death and resurrection. All the sacraments are means to develop the life begun at Baptism.

Make a list of things your family will do this week to be a sign to others that by Baptism each of us has been freed from the power of original sin and empowered to do God's will. Write what you will do this week to show you are water, or new life, to someone.

† Family Prayer

Play recorded music that will help your family reflect upon water as a source of life. Ask each family member to think prayerfully about her or his Baptism. Then, two at a time, go to a prayer table on which some holy water and a large copy of this blessing have been placed. Take turns blessing one another. Make the sign of the cross on one another's forehead while saying,

"May God the Holy Spirit help you to fulfill the promises of your Baptism."

Learn by heart Faith Summary

● We receive new life at Baptism when we are reborn of water and the Holy Spirit.

● At Baptism we are initiated into, or begin to become members of the Church, the body of Christ.

● Our Baptism calls us to decide to live for the reign of God.

Bringing New Life to Others

Review

Go over the *Faith Summary* together. Encourage your fifth grader to learn it by heart, especially the first two statements. Then have him or her do the *Review*. The answers to numbers 1–4 appear on page 216. The response to number 5 will help you to see how well your fifth grader is growing in living the promises made at Baptism. When the *Review* is completed, go over it together.

Circle the letter beside the correct answer.

1. The most important sign of Baptism is
   a. oil.
   b. water.
   c. a white garment.
   d. a candle.

2. At Baptism we are initiated into, or become members of,
   a. our family.
   b. the body of Christ.
   c. our country.
   d. our neighborhood.

3. The Christian community, the Church,
   a. welcomes us as members.
   b. uses the sign of water in Baptism.
   c. is the body of Christ.
   d. all of these

4. We can live our Baptism by
   a. trying to live our Christian faith.
   b. avoiding people who need help.
   c. ignoring those who hurt us.
   d. not taking part in Mass.

5. In what way will you carry on the work of Jesus Christ in the world?

_____

_____

_____

FAMILY SCRIPTURE MOMENT

Gather and ask: What experiences have we had that made us feel new or renewed? Then **Listen** as Jesus reveals a surprising truth.

One night Nicodemus, a leader of the people, went to Jesus and said, "Rabbi, we know that You are a teacher sent by God." Jesus answered, "No one can see the kingdom of God without being born again." "How can a grown person be born again?" Nicodemus asked. "I am telling you the truth," replied Jesus, "that no one can enter the kingdom of God without being born of water and the Spirit. A person is born physically of human parents, but is born spiritually of the Spirit."

From John 3:2–6

Share what each one understands by the phrase "being born again of water and the Spirit."

Consider for family enrichment:

■ Although Nicodemus was a deeply religious person, he did not understand that Jesus' disciples had to be born "from above," or from the Spirit.

■ By our Baptism, we have been born "of water and the Spirit" and have received a share in God's own life. We have become members of the Church, the body of Christ.

Reflect and **Decide** Invite family members to picture themselves at the moment of their Baptism. Ask: How will we show that we have been born of the Holy Spirit?

9 Jesus Christ Strengthens Us
(Confirmation)

Come, Holy
Spirit,
strengthen us
to be Christ's
witnesses.

OUR LIFE

The early missionaries to North America
faced many dangers. One day in 1642
Father Isaac Jogues was ambushed by the
Iroquois, the enemies of the Hurons, and
tortured as a hostage for one year.

Instead of returning home after being
ransomed, Father Jogues assumed the role of
a peacemaker between the Hurons and the
Iroquois. Once again, he was taken hostage.
This time he and seven other French
missionaries were killed.

In 1930 the Church canonized these martyrs
as saints. They are called the North
American Martyrs. The word *martyr* means
witness.

Why do you think Father Jogues stayed in
North America?

Tell some of the ways that you give witness
to your Christian faith today.
Who helps you?

SHARING LIFE

Talk together about the following questions.

What are some of the things that make it
difficult for you to be a Christian?

What in our society makes it difficult for
anyone to be a good Christian?

How do you imagine you could be a better
witness to your Christian faith?

Sending of the Holy Spirit

It is not always easy to be a witness to our faith. We need God's special help.

At the Last Supper on the night before He died, Jesus knew that His disciples would be afraid and feel lost without Him. Jesus tried to give them courage by promising, "I will ask God to give you another Helper, who will stay with you forever."

From John 14:16

After Jesus ascended into heaven, His disciples became frightened and locked themselves in an upper room. They were afraid of being found and arrested.

Ten days later, while they were still huddled there, God the Holy Spirit came. Each disciple was blessed with the fullness of the Holy Spirit and received the gifts that we receive in the sacrament of Confirmation. Jesus had kept His promise to send the Holy Spirit.

Now they became fearless and ready to give witness to their faith in Jesus. They ran into the streets and began to preach the good news of Jesus to everyone they met.

From Acts 1:7–14; 2:1–13

Our Church calls this day Pentecost. On that day God the Holy Spirit came upon the first Christian disciples. They now had the courage to invite others to believe in and to follow Jesus.

Confirmation, A Sacrament of Initiation

In Confirmation we receive the sign, or seal, of the Holy Spirit. This seal is not visible, but it marks us as followers and witnesses of Christ.

When we were baptized, we began our initiation into the Church. Confirmation is one more step in this initiation into the body of Christ. Now we are called to give public witness to the good news to our family, our neighbors, and even strangers. We are sealed with the Gift of the Holy Spirit and strengthened to live out our baptismal promises.

When we are confirmed, we may choose another name in addition to the one we

Holy oil

Holy Spirit

Holy

FAITH WORD

Confirmation is the sacrament in which we are sealed with the Gift of the Holy Spirit and are strengthened to give witness to the good news of Jesus.

were given at Baptism. We may select the name of a saint whose life we have read about and whom we admire.

Confirmation is celebrated during Mass with a bishop or his representative presiding. A high point of the celebration of Confirmation is the "laying on of hands." The bishop extends his hands over those to be confirmed, praying in part,

"Send your Holy Spirit upon them
to be their Helper and Guide.
Give them the spirit of wisdom and
    understanding,
the spirit of right judgment and courage,
the spirit of knowledge and reverence.

Fill them with the spirit of wonder and awe
    in your presence."

Then the bishop dips his thumb into blessed oil, called holy chrism. He makes the sign of the cross on their foreheads and anoints them, saying,

"(*Name*), be sealed with the Gift of the Holy Spirit."

This anointing is the most important sign of the sacrament of Confirmation.

Confirmation helps us to practice our faith openly and bravely, no matter who makes fun of us or how difficult it may be.

The Holy Spirit helps us so that other people will see the good news of Jesus alive in us. They will know by our actions that God loves every human being.

When we live our Confirmation, we become witnesses to the reign of God in the world today.

Coming to Faith

After your Confirmation, what would you tell others about:

● the promises Jesus gave His disciples;

● the coming of the Holy Spirit;

● the important signs used at Confirmation;

● how you can be a better Christian witness to others?

Practicing Faith

†Gather in a circle and pray together.

All: Come, Holy Spirit, be our Helper and Guide. (Repeat after each petition.) (All hold out arms to center of circle, palms down as seven people read.)

1. Give us Your gift of wisdom so we may know the right thing to do. (All)

2. Give us Your gift of understanding so our faith will be real and deep. (All)

3. Give us Your gift of right judgment so that we may help others in their faith. (All)

4. Give us Your gift of courage so we may practice what we believe with courage. (All)

5. Give us Your gift of knowledge so that we may desire to learn all we can about our faith. (All)

6. Give us Your gift of reverence so that we may be people of prayer and worship. (All)

7. Give us Your gift of wonder and awe so that we may treat all people and all creation with respect and wonder. (All)

Close by singing
"Come, Holy Spirit."

Talk with your catechist about ways you and your family might use the "Faith Alive" pages. You might especially want to pray together the prayer to the Holy Spirit.

FAITH ALIVE AT HOME AND IN THE PARISH

In this lesson your fifth grader has learned more about the sacrament of Confirmation. In this sacrament the baptized are sealed with the Gift of the Holy Spirit. The Holy Spirit helps us live our faith by giving us special gifts and fruits. (See the chart below.)

Gifts of the Spirit

The gifts of the Holy Spirit are listed below. Choose one gift of the Holy Spirit. Discuss how you and your family will live it this week.

Fruits of the Spirit

The fruits of the Holy Spirit are the good results people can see in us when we use the gifts of the Holy Spirit. These fruits are *love, joy, peace, patience, kindness, goodness, faithfulness, humility,* and *self-control*.

Discuss with your fifth grader ways you see the fruits of the Spirit at home or in your parish.

† Family Prayer to the Holy Spirit

Holy Spirit, we thank You for Your gifts. We ask Your guidance for our family and parish. (Place hands on each family member.)

Learn by heart Faith Summary

- Confirmation is the sacrament in which we are sealed with the Gift of the Holy Spirit and strengthened to give witness to the good news of Jesus Christ.

- In Confirmation the Holy Spirit fills us with the gifts that we need to live our Christian faith.

- We live our Confirmation when we become witnesses to the reign of God in the world.

Gift	Helps us to
wisdom	know the right things to do.
understanding	explain our faith and know how to make good decisions.
right judgment	guide others in their faith because we live our own.
courage	practice courageously the faith we believe.
knowledge	learn about our Catholic faith from the Bible and from the Catholic tradition.
reverence	live the good news willingly and pray for ourselves and others.
wonder and awe	show respect for God, God's people, and God's world.

Review

Go over the *Faith Summary* together and encourage your fifth grader to learn it by heart, especially the first statement. Then have him or her do the *Review*. The answers to numbers 1–4 appear on page 216. The response to number 5 will help you to see how well your fifth grader understands our responsibility to live as witnesses to Jesus' mission. When the *Review* is completed, go over it together.

Circle the letter beside the correct answer.

1. At Confirmation we receive
   a. the gift of new life.
   b. freedom from original sin.
   c. the power to forgive sins.
   d. the fullness of the Holy Spirit.

2. The person who leads the Confirmation celebration is
   a. the bishop or his representative.
   b. the priest.
   c. our parents.
   d. the disciples.

3. The sign, or seal, of the Holy Spirit
   a. is visible.
   b. lasts only for the Confirmation ceremony.
   c. marks us forever as followers of Christ.
   d. is the bishop.

4. At Confirmation we accept the responsibility to
   a. live our baptismal promises.
   b. practice our faith openly.
   c. become witnesses to the reign of God.
   d. all of these

5. How will you give witness as a Christian this week?

_____

_____

_____

FAMILY SCRIPTURE MOMENT

Gather and have family members recall times when they wanted to speak up about what they believe, but did not do so. Then **Listen** to an important message about the Holy Spirit.

Jesus said, "When the Spirit comes, who reveals the truth about God, the Spirit will lead you into all the truth. This will be done on the Spirit's own authority. The Spirit will tell you of things to come. The Spirit will give Me glory, because the Spirit will take what I say and tell it to you. All that My Father has is Mine; that is why I said that the Spirit will take what I give and tell it to you."

From John 16:13–15

Share Ask: What kind of witnesses to our faith would we like to be? How can the Holy Spirit help us?

Consider for family enrichment:
■ At the Last Supper, Jesus promises that the Spirit will give Him glory by enabling the disciples to know and live the truth.

■ At Confirmation we receive the Spirit's gifts that enable us to become witnesses to the good news of Jesus.

Reflect and **Decide** How do we need to grow as disciples who speak up about Jesus? When will our family pray for the help of the Holy Spirit?

10 | Jesus Christ Feeds Us
(Eucharist)

Jesus, Living
Bread, fill us
with Your life.

Our Life

Once the people asked Jesus what miracle He would do so that they might believe in Him. Jesus said, "I am the Bread of Life: He who comes to Me will never be hungry; he who believes in Me will never be thirsty."

The people started grumbling. They said, "This is Joseph's son, isn't He? How can He talk like this?"

Jesus answered, "Stop muttering among yourselves. I am telling you the truth. I am the Bread of Life.... I am the living Bread that came down from heaven. Anyone who eats this Bread will live forever. The Bread that I will give is My flesh so that the world may live."

At this an angry argument began. "How can this man give us His flesh to eat?" they asked. But Jesus quietly repeated what He had said. Many of His followers who heard Him said, "This teaching is too hard. Who can believe it?" They turned away and walked with Him no more.

From John 6:35, 41–43, 47–53, 60, 66

What do you hear Jesus saying in this Scripture story?

Sharing Life

Why do you think Jesus compared Himself to bread?

Discuss together: Why are there so many hungry people in our world?

What do you think Jesus wants us to do for people who are hungry?

The Eucharist, A Sacrament of Initiation

Sometimes we share a meal not only because we are hungry, but also because we are celebrating a special event like Thanksgiving or a birthday.

At Passover the Jewish people celebrate an important meal to remember that God brought them from slavery in Egypt to freedom in the Promised Land. During Passover, on the night before He died, Jesus ate a very special meal with His friends. This meal is called the Last Supper.

At this Last Supper Jesus gave us the gift of Himself, His own Body and Blood. Jesus' disciples never forgot this meal. This is what happened.

"The Lord Jesus, on the night He was betrayed, took a piece of bread, gave thanks to God, broke it, and said, 'This is My Body, which is for you. Do this in memory of Me.' In the same way, after the supper He took a cup of wine and said, 'This cup is God's new covenant, sealed with My blood. Whenever you drink it, do so in memory of Me.'"

From 1 Corinthians 11:23–25

At the Last Supper Jesus gave thanks to God. Ordinary bread and wine became His own Body and Blood. Then Jesus asked His disciples to do the same in memory of Him. We call this the *Eucharist*, a word that means "to give thanks."

The Eucharist is both a sacrifice and a meal. In the Eucharist we share in the one sacrifice of Christ. We give thanks and celebrate Jesus' death and resurrection. In this sacrifice of praise to God, we remember all that Jesus did for us. In the Eucharist we offer ourselves with Jesus to God.

The sacrament of the Eucharist is also a community meal. In this sacrament we receive the gift of Jesus, who gave Himself to

us as our food. Jesus is really present in the Eucharist. Sharing in the Eucharist makes us one with God and with one another in the Church, the body of Christ.

We assemble as Jesus' community of disciples to celebrate the Eucharist at Mass. We remember that Jesus loved us so much that He sacrificed Himself for us and died on the cross to save us from our sins. Through the Eucharist we become a living sacrifice of praise.

We remember that Jesus rose from the dead and now remains with us in the Eucharist. We give thanks to Jesus for the gift of Himself by living as His disciples.

FAITH WORD

The **Eucharist** is the sacrament of Jesus' Body and Blood. Jesus is really present in the Eucharist.

Thanking God for Jesus

At Mass our gifts of bread and wine become the Body and Blood of Christ. This happens through the power of the Holy Spirit. Jesus is really present under the appearances of bread and wine.

Our participation in Mass is a sign of our full initiation into the Church, the body of Christ. The Eucharist nourishes us to give thanks to God by living as God's own people. In Holy Communion we receive Jesus Himself. He is our Bread of Life. We can also visit our parish church and pray to Jesus, who is present in the Blessed Sacrament.

Saint Augustine once said, "Because we receive the Body of Christ in Holy Communion, we must live as the body of Christ in the world." We can share Jesus, our Bread of Life, by:

- caring for the hungry by organizing food collections in our parish.
- sharing Jesus' joy by visiting a lonely or elderly person.
- welcoming a newcomer into our group or neighborhood.
  - being kind to someone whom others treat badly.
    - being careful not to waste food or drink when many other people are so hungry.
      - being kind and patient with our family and friends.

TIHSEIBNRME EAMDOORFYL OIFFMEE

I AM

_____

COMING TO FAITH

Decode the message from Jesus about the Eucharist. Beginning with the first letter in the lines of letters, circle every other letter to find the message. Then write the message.

Discuss together the best way to explain the sacrament of the Eucharist to a young person who is not a Catholic.

PRACTICING FAITH

How can you show that you *really* believe that Jesus is present in the Eucharist? Remember, belief is expressed in action. Some ideas are listed on page 71. Your group might come up with your own. Make a group plan about how and when you will share Jesus, our Bread of Life, this week. Write your plan.

Close by praying the prayer on page 73.

Talk with your catechist about ways you and your family might use the "Faith Alive" pages. You might especially want to invite a family member to make a visit to the Blessed Sacrament.

This lesson on the Eucharist is an opportunity for your family to renew the central place this wonderful sacrament has in our Catholic faith. Saint Thomas Aquinas called the Eucharist "the sacrament of sacraments"—the greatest sacrament of all! Read with your family the words of Jesus in which He describes Himself as the Bread of Life (John 6:35–61). Discuss what the words of Jesus from this story might mean for your family today.

The Blessed Sacrament is another name for the Eucharist. After Mass, the Blessed Sacrament is usually kept, or reserved, in the tabernacle in a special place in the church. This is done so that Holy Communion may be brought to the sick of our parish, and so that we may worship Jesus truly present in the Blessed Sacrament.

To deepen your love and the love of your family for the gift of the Eucharist, make a visit together this week to Jesus in the Blessed Sacrament.

† **Family Prayer**

Jesus, be with us and with our
   parish family.
Remind us to share our lives
   as bread for others;
help us to share our joys
   as wine for others.

Learn by heart **Faith Summary**

- The Eucharist is the sacrament of the Body and Blood of Christ.
- Jesus is the Bread of Life. The food that Jesus gives us is His own Body and Blood.
- We respond to the gift of the Eucharist by living for the reign of God.

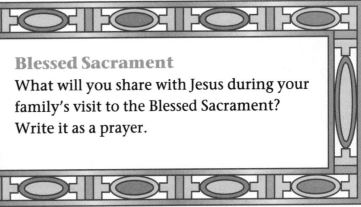

Blessed Sacrament
What will you share with Jesus during your family's visit to the Blessed Sacrament? Write it as a prayer.

Review

Go over the *Faith Summary* together and encourage your fifth grader to learn it by heart, especially the first two statements. Then have him or her do the *Review*. The answers to numbers 1–4 appear on page 216. The response to number 5 will show how well your fifth grader is growing in his or her love for the Eucharist. When the *Review* is completed, go over it together.

Circle the letter beside the correct answer.

1. Jesus celebrated the first Eucharist
   a. after His death.
   b. by Himself.
   c. for Himself.
   d. during a feast of Passover.

2. When we receive the Eucharist,
   a. we eat Jesus' Body and drink His Blood.
   b. we receive only bread and wine.
   c. we always celebrate alone.
   d. we do not need to receive it again.

3. The word *Eucharist* means
   a. "Last Supper."
   b. "bread and wine."
   c. "to give thanks."
   d. "blessed be God."

4. We receive Jesus Himself, as our Bread of Life, in
   a. Baptism.
   b. Holy Communion.
   c. Confirmation.
   d. the Last Supper.

5. What one thing will you do this week to show that you are thankful for the Eucharist?

_____

_____

_____

_____

FAMILY SCRIPTURE MOMENT

Gather and ask: What does food do for us? What "foods" nourish our spirits? Then **Listen** as a family to the words of Jesus.

"I am telling you the truth," Jesus said. "What Moses gave you was not the bread from heaven; it is My Father who gives you the real bread from heaven. For the bread that God gives is He who comes down from heaven and gives life to the world." "Sir," they asked Him, "give us this bread always." "I am the Bread of Life," Jesus told them. "Whoever comes to Me will never be hungry; whoever believes in Me will never be thirsty. I will never turn away anyone who comes to Me."

John 6:32–35, 37

Share what each one heard Jesus saying.

Consider for family enrichment:

■ Jesus tells the crowd that the real bread from heaven is not the manna God provided for Moses and the people who wandered in the desert. Jesus Himself is the Bread of Life sent by God.

■ We can bring all our spiritual hungers to the Eucharist and are nourished by the real presence of Christ.

Reflect and **Decide** What might we do as a family to increase our appreciation for the Eucharist and to live it this week?

74

11 | Our Church Celebrates the Eucharist
(The Mass)

Lamb of God, You take away the sins of the world, grant us peace.

OUR LIFE

The parish is having a big farewell party for Mr. Sandro. He has been a catechist in the parish for five years, and now he is leaving to work as a lay missionary in Central America.

The fifth graders are sad. Mr. Sandro has been their catechist for two years. He has also been their friend. Two years is a long time. They wonder whether he will forget them.

Mr. Sandro says goodbye. He tells them that sharing faith with them was wonderful for him. He says, "I'll always remember you— each one of you!"

Is there someone who has been a special person in your life? Who? How?

How would you say goodbye to that person? How would you remember that person?

SHARING LIFE

Discuss together.

Do you have memories of someone important to you to whom you had to say goodbye?

Tell how the memory of that person makes a difference in your life.

How does remembering Jesus make a difference in your life now?

What do you think is the best way to remember Jesus?

Our Catholic Faith

Celebrating Mass

The Mass is our celebration of the Eucharist. Every Sunday or Saturday evening, the Catholic community gathers together as a worshiping assembly. We do this to remember the life, death, and resurrection of Jesus. At Mass we praise and honor God.

The two major parts of the Mass are the Liturgy of the Word and the Liturgy of the Eucharist.

In the Introductory Rites we begin our Mass with an opening song and greeting. We ask God and one another for forgiveness in the Penitential Rite. Then we praise God and pray for the strength to live for God's reign.

Liturgy of the Word

God speaks to us in the Liturgy of the Word. Selections from the Old and New Testaments are read aloud from the Bible by the reader, deacon, or priest.

The Responsorial Psalm follows the first reading. Praying this psalm response helps us to make a connection between our lives and the Old Testament reading.

The first New Testament reading is from one of the Letters, also called Epistles, or from the Acts of the Apostles or the Book of Revelation.

We prepare for the gospel proclamation by standing and singing the Alleluia. *Alleluia* is a Hebrew word meaning "praise to God."

The deacon or priest then proclaims the good news of Jesus from one of the four gospels: Matthew, Mark, Luke, or John.

After the gospel the priest or deacon gives a homily, or sermon, about the readings. This helps us to live God's word in our world today. After the homily we profess our common faith by saying the Creed together.

The Liturgy of the Word concludes with the Prayer of the Faithful. We pray for our own needs, the needs of others, the needs of the Church, and the needs of the whole world.

Liturgy of the Eucharist

The Liturgy of the Eucharist begins with the Preparation of the Gifts. Members of the assembly bring our gifts of bread and wine to the altar. These gifts are signs that we are returning to God the gift of our lives. They are also signs of our efforts to care for one another and all of God's creation.

Liturgy is the official public worship of the Church. The Liturgy includes the ways we celebrate the Mass and other sacraments.

We stand as the priest invites us to join in the Eucharistic Prayer. This is our Church's great prayer of praise and thanks to God for all creation and for our salvation. We respond with the "Holy, holy, holy, Lord" prayer.

Then the priest says and does what Jesus did at the Last Supper. Taking the bread, the priest prays, "Take this, all of you, and eat it: this is my body which will be given up for you."

Taking the chalice, he continues, "Take this, all of you, and drink from it: this is the cup of my blood, the blood of the new and everlasting covenant. It will be shed for you and for all so that sins may be forgiven. Do this in memory of me."

Through the power of the Holy Spirit and the words and actions of the priest, the bread and wine become Jesus' own Body and Blood. We call this the consecration.

After proclaiming the mystery of faith and the Great Amen, we prepare for Holy Communion by saying or singing the Our Father. We pray for God's forgiveness and then share a sign of peace with those around us.

While praying the Lamb of God prayer, the priest breaks the consecrated Host. This is a sign that we share in the one Bread of Life.

The priest receives Holy Communion. The members of the community next share Jesus' Body and Blood. We may receive the Host in our hand or on our tongue. We may also be invited to receive Communion from the chalice.

The priest or eucharistic minister says to us, "The body of Christ," and if we receive from the chalice, "The blood of Christ." We respond "Amen." Our Amen means that we believe Jesus is really present with us in the Eucharist and in our lives.

In the Concluding Rite the priest blesses us. He or the deacon sends us forth, and says, "Go in peace to love and serve the Lord."

Through the Mass, we receive the grace to live as true members of the Church, the body of Christ. We are nourished to be the sacrament of God's reign in the world.

COMING TO FAITH

Explain why the Mass is the greatest celebration for God's people.

Put a "W" for the parts of the Mass in the Liturgy of the Word. Put an "E" for the parts of the Mass in the Liturgy of the Eucharist. Then number each part in the order in which it occurs.

Letter	Number	
_____	_____	Sign of Peace
_____	_____	Gospel
_____	_____	"This is my body."
_____	_____	"This is the cup of my blood."
_____	_____	Homily/Sermon
_____	_____	Epistle/Letter
_____	_____	Consecration
_____	_____	Lord's Prayer

PRACTICING FAITH

Talk together about ways you can live as the body of Christ in the world. For example:

- serve, be a helper, in your parish
- find ways to help the poor, the homeless
- be aware of and respond to injustices
- be peacemakers at home, in your parish, in your neighborhood

Plan what your group will try to do this week. Then pray the prayer of Saint Francis together (page 205).

Talk with your catechist about ways you and your family might use the "Faith Alive" pages. You might plan to go to Mass together as a family this week.

FAITH ALIVE AT HOME AND IN THE PARISH

In this lesson your fifth grader has learned in more detail about the actual celebration of the Mass. The Mass is our greatest celebration and sign that we are the body of Christ in the world. Saint Paul wrote, "We are sharing in the Body and Blood of Christ. Because there is the one loaf of bread, all of us, though many, are one body, for we all share the same loaf."

From 1 Corinthians 10:16–17

The laws of the Church require Catholics to participate in the Mass on Sunday or Saturday evening and on certain other holy days of obligation. This is a serious responsibility. Sometimes, however, our participation can become routine and thoughtless. Talk together as a family about what you will do to share more fully and responsively in the Mass. Be sure to discuss the reasons for worshiping together that go far beyond the level of obligation. Focus on the privilege of coming together as a community of faith to praise and thank God.

† Family Prayer

Pray this prayer each morning.

Jesus, help us to know what You want us to do for others today.

Learn by heart Faith Summary

- The two major parts of the Mass are the Liturgy of the Word and the Liturgy of the Eucharist.

- During the Liturgy of the Word, we listen to God's word from the Bible.

- During the Liturgy of the Eucharist, our gifts of bread and wine become the Body and Blood of Christ.

Remember our call to live the Eucharist by loving and serving the Lord all week long.

Before Mass we will...

_____

_____

We will "live" the Mass by...

_____

_____

During Mass we will...

_____

_____

Review

Go over the *Faith Summary* together and encourage your fifth grader to learn it by heart, especially the first statement. Then have him or her do the *Review*. The answers to numbers 1–4 appear on page 216. The response to number 5 will help you to see how well your fifth grader is growing in appreciation of the Mass as our Church's greatest prayer. When the *Review* is completed, go over it together.

Circle the letter beside the correct answer.

1. The celebration of the Eucharist is
   a. the rosary.
   b. the Lord's prayer.
   c. the Mass.
   d. the Gospel.

2. At Mass we hear God's word read from the Bible during the
   a. Introductory Rites.
   b. Liturgy of the Word.
   c. Liturgy of the Eucharist.
   d. Concluding Rite.

3. The central part of the Liturgy of the Eucharist is
   a. the Eucharistic Prayer.
   b. the Our Father.
   c. the "Holy, holy, holy, Lord" prayer.
   d. the "Lamb of God" prayer.

4. At Mass the bread and wine become Jesus' own Body and Blood during the
   a. Liturgy of the Word.
   b. Holy Communion.
   c. Lord's Prayer.
   d. Eucharistic Prayer.

5. What will you thank God for at Mass next Sunday or Saturday evening?

_____

_____

_____

FAMILY SCRIPTURE MOMENT

Gather and ask: what does it mean for us to worship God? Then **Listen** as a family.

A Samaritan woman came to draw water from the well, and Jesus said to her, "Give me a drink of water." The woman answered, "You are a Jew, and I am a Samaritan—so how can You ask me for a drink?" Jesus answered, "Whoever drinks this water will get thirsty again. The water that I will give will become a spring which will give eternal life. But the time is coming and is already here, when by the power of God's Spirit people will worship the Father in Spirit and truth."
From John 4:7, 9, 13–14, 23

Share what each person hears Jesus saying in this conversation with the Samaritan woman.

Consider for family enrichment:

■ By sharing the truth about Himself as the source of life-giving water, Jesus reveals that in Him all people can offer true worship to God.

■ At Mass we worship and give thanks to the Father, through the Son, in the Holy Spirit. It is our true worship "in Spirit and truth."

Reflect and **Decide** How can our worship influence our daily lives? Pray: Loving Creator, by the power of the Holy Spirit, who sanctifies us, and with Your Son, who redeems us, we worship You and give You thanks.

12 The Church Remembers
(Liturgical Year)

Thank You, God, for the gift of time. Help us to use it in Your service.

A wise teacher in the Old Testament once wrote:

There is a season for everything, a time for everything under heaven: a time for being born, a time for dying, a time for planting, a time for harvesting, a time for tears, a time for laughter, a time for grieving, a time for dancing.

From Ecclesiastes 3:1, 4

These words tell us that there is a season, a time, for everything. Talk about your favorite time of the year.

How is each time different and special?

How does each season prepare us, and the world, for the next season?

SHARING LIFE

Are there "seasons," times of change, in our human lives?

Discuss why we have times for planting and harvesting, for tears and for laughter, for grieving and for rejoicing.

At what time is God with us? How?

OUR CATHOLIC FAITH

The Liturgical Year

Our Church has seasons that make up our liturgical year to remind us of Jesus' life, death, and resurrection. These seasons help us to remember that all time is a holy time to be lived in the presence of God.

Advent Season

The liturgical year begins with the four weeks of the Advent season, immediately before Christmas. During this time, we remember that the Jewish people waited and hoped for a Messiah. We wait and hope for the coming of Jesus at Christmas and at the end of time.

Christmas Season

The Christmas season celebrates the birth of Jesus and the announcement to the world that He is the Messiah promised by God.

Lenten Season

The season of Lent is a time of preparation for Easter and for the renewal of our Baptism. Lent begins on Ash Wednesday and lasts for forty days. It is a time to remember the words of Jesus, "The reign of God is near! Turn away from your sins and believe the good news" (from Mark 1:15).

Catholics for centuries have prepared for Easter in special ways during Lent. Adults *fast*, or eat less and do without snacks between meals, on Ash Wednesday and Good Friday.

Those fourteen or older *abstain*, or do not eat meat, on Ash Wednesday and the Fridays of Lent. We do without things so that we can have more to share with the poor.

Passion, or Palm, Sunday is the last Sunday of Lent and the first day of Holy Week.

Easter Triduum

The Easter Triduum, or "three days," is the most important time of the entire Church year. It begins with the Mass of the Lord's Supper on Holy Thursday evening and continues through Good Friday and the Easter Vigil on Holy Saturday. It concludes with Evening Prayer on Easter Sunday. During these three days we remember the Last Supper and Jesus' gift of Himself in the Eucharist. We recall His passion and death on the cross. We celebrate His resurrection.

Annunciazione, Domenico Ghirlandaio, (15th century)

Easter Season

On Easter Sunday, the greatest feast of the liturgical year, we celebrate Jesus' resurrection and our new life with God. The Easter season continues for fifty days until Pentecost Sunday.

On Pentecost we remember the day the Holy Spirit came to Jesus' first disciples. We recall that without the Holy Spirit we could not live as God's people.

Ordinary Time

The weeks of the year that are not part of the seasons of Advent, Christmas, Lent, the Triduum, or Easter are known as Ordinary Time. The Church reminds us that God is always with us and present in our lives, no matter what the time.

Feast Days

Many feast days are celebrated during the liturgical year. The chart shows some of the feast days on which we remember the lives of Jesus, Mary, and the saints.

Advent Season
Immaculate Conception,
   December 8
Our Lady of Guadalupe,
   December 12

Christmas Season
Christmas, December 25
Mary, Mother of God, January 1
Epiphany

Ordinary Time
Presentation of the Lord, February 2

Lenten Season
Ash Wednesday
Joseph, Husband of Mary, March 19
Annunciation, March 25
Passion, or Palm, Sunday

Easter Triduum
Passion, death, and resurrection
   of the Lord

Easter Season
Easter
Ascension
Pentecost

Ordinary Time
Assumption, August 15
Birth of Mary, September 8
All Saints, November 1
All Souls, November 2
Christ the King

Coming To Faith

How would you explain the liturgical year to a fourth grader?

With a team, make up a key word for each season. Share your key words with the whole group.

Practicing Faith

†Gather in a prayer circle.

Reader 1: Loving God, we thank You for the gift of time.

All: (Response) Thank You for Your presence with us always.

Reader 2: For Advent, when we take time to prepare for the coming again of Your divine Son. (Response)

Reader 3: For Christmas, when we celebrate the birth of our Savior. (Response)

Reader 4: For Lent, when we do penance and grow as disciples of Jesus. (Response)

Reader 5: For the Easter Triduum, when we celebrate the death and resurrection of Jesus. (Response)

Reader 6: For the Easter season, when we rejoice in the new life of the risen Christ. (Response)

Reader 7: For Ordinary Time, which reminds us that You are with us in the everyday events of our lives. (Response)

Now pray the Glory to the Father prayer. Then take turns and pray:
Loving God, in this season of _____, help us to live as disciples of Jesus by

_____.

Talk with your catechist about ways you and your family might use the "Faith Alive" pages. You might especially want to find time to do the activity together.

FAITH ALIVE AT HOME AND IN THE PARISH

By celebrating the Church's liturgical year, we encounter the story of our faith over and over again. Jesus' life, death, and resurrection is the heart of the story. The stories of Mary and the other saints give us many examples of the way to live each day as disciples of Jesus Christ. The liturgical year reminds us that all time is sacred and is permeated with the presence of God.

Our identity as Catholics is strongly influenced by the rituals we celebrate in our parish and home during Advent, Christmas, Lent, and Easter. We have a wealth of feast days on which to celebrate the life of Christ and the lives of Mary and the other saints. Some Catholics, remembering Good Friday, keep the custom of not eating meat on Fridays throughout the year. All of these experiences can enrich our spiritual lives by drawing us each year into the cycle of our common faith story.

Do the activity below to help your fifth grader appreciate the liturgical year. Then pray the family prayer together.

† Family Prayer

Leader: Let us praise the Lord of days and seasons and years, saying: Glory to God in the highest!

Family: And peace to God's people on earth!

Our lives are made of days and nights, of seasons and years, for we are a part of our universe. We mark ends, and we make beginnings, and we praise God for the grace and mercy that fills our days. Amen.

The Liturgical Seasons

Make a five-sided diagram like this one to illustrate the liturgical seasons.

Learn by heart Faith Summary

● The liturgical seasons of the Church year are Advent, Christmas, Lent, the Easter Triduum, Easter, and Ordinary Time.

● During the liturgical year we also honor and pray to Mary and the other saints.

● The liturgical year reminds us that we always live in the presence of God.

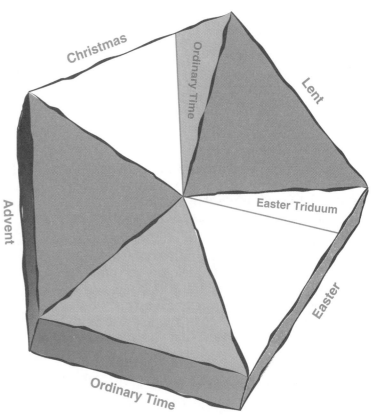

Review

Go over the *Faith Summary* together and encourage your fifth grader to learn it by heart, especially the first statement. Then have him or her do the *Review*. The answers to numbers 1–4 appear on page 216. The response to number 5 will show you how well your fifth grader understands the different liturgical seasons of the Church year. When the *Review* is completed, go over it together.

Circle the letter beside the correct answer.

1. The liturgical year begins with the season of
   a. Advent.
   b. Christmas.
   c. Lent.
   d. Easter.

2. Which is NOT a liturgical season?
   a. Advent
   b. Ordinary Time
   c. Easter Season
   d. feast of the Immaculate Conception

3. The most important time in the Church year is
   a. Ordinary Time.
   b. the Easter Triduum.
   c. Lent.
   d. Christmas.

4. The season of the liturgical year during which we prepare for Easter is
   a. Advent.
   b. Christmas.
   c. Lent.
   d. Ordinary Time.

5. What will you do to celebrate the present liturgical season?

_____

_____

_____

_____

FAMILY SCRIPTURE MOMENT

Gather and ask: What everyday clues have we observed that God is present in our lives? Then **Listen** as Jesus prays for His disciples at the Last Supper.

"Father, the hour has come. Give glory to Your Son, so that the Son may give glory to You. I have made You known to those You gave Me out of the world. They have obeyed Your word. I gave them the message that You gave Me, and they received it; they know that it is true that I came from You, and they believe that You sent Me. Keep them safe by the power of Your name, so that they may be one just as You and I are one."

From John 17:1, 6, 8, 11

Share Ask: What is Jesus' message for us? What is Jesus' prayer for us?

Consider for family enrichment:

■ Jesus expresses His love for His friends by praying that they will experience the same loving unity He enjoys with the Father.

■ Jesus always intercedes for us that we may one day inherit the kingdom. Surely, Jesus' prayer is answered.

Reflect and **Decide** How does living in harmony with the Church year help us to be one with God and one another? What will we as a family do to celebrate the present liturgical season?

13 | Celebrating Advent

Hail Mary, full of grace, the Lord is with you.

Our Life

Here is an old legend that might have something true to say to us today.

Once long ago three children were playing in their garden. A messenger came along the road. "The king will pass this way today," he announced. The children were so excited. "Perhaps the king will stop by our garden! Let's make it beautiful!" So the children worked to make their garden beautiful, and they made sure they had fruit and bread and cool drinks. Then they waited... and waited...and waited.
It was almost sunset when an old man stopped at their garden wall. "What a beautiful garden," he said. "It looks so shady and cool. May I come in and rest awhile?"

The children did not know what to do. They were waiting for the king! But then—the poor man looked so tired and hungry. "Come in," they said and they had him sit in the shade and they brought him food and drink. Then they told him that they had worked to make everything ready for the king. But the king hadn't come. They were so disappointed.

Suddenly a lovely light shone around the man. He wasn't old or shabby anymore. He was handsome. He smiled at the children. "Your king *did* pass today," he said, "and you welcomed him."

Share what you learned from this story for your own life.

Sharing Life

Discuss together: what are the ways that Jesus comes into our lives today?

How can we recognize Him?

Talk about ways we might get ready for His coming.

Our Catholic Faith

Waiting for a Savior

Hundreds of years before Jesus was born, a prophet named Isaiah told the Israelites many things about the promised Savior, or Messiah, for whom they were waiting. Isaiah told the people that the Savior would be born of a young woman who would name him Immanuel. *Immanuel* means "God with us."

Isaiah said that the Savior would rule the people of Israel wisely. Isaiah wrote, "The spirit of God will give him wisdom and the knowledge and the skill to rule his people" (from Isaiah 11:2).

Isaiah also described the Savior as a descendant of David, who was Israel's best loved king. The Messiah would be the great champion of justice. Isaiah told the Israelites, "He will rule as David's successor, basing his power on right and justice from now until the end of time" (Isaiah 9:7).

Isaiah also said that the child born to be their Savior would be called "Wonderful Counselor, Mighty God, Prince of Peace" (Isaiah 9:6).

Like Isaiah, the other writers of the Bible often compared sin to darkness. At the time of Isaiah, many Israelites had turned away from God and were living in the darkness of sin. Isaiah compared the coming of the Savior to the breaking forth of light in darkness. The prophet said, "The people who walked in darkness have seen a great light. They lived in a land of shadows but now light is shining on them" (Isaiah 9:2).

Isaiah also told the Israelites that they could recognize the Savior by his works. The Savior

would help the poor, heal the sick, and free the oppressed (From Isaiah 61:1–2).

The Coming of the Savior

Israel waited in hope for the coming of the promised Savior.

Many years after Isaiah, the angel Gabriel was sent to the Virgin Mary in the town of Nazareth in Galilee. The angel told her, "You will give birth to a Son, and He will be called the Son of the Most High God. The Lord God will make Him a King, as His ancestor David was" (Luke 1:26–33).

During Advent we remember the words of Isaiah and think about what they mean for us today. We prepare for the feast of Christmas and for Jesus' coming again. We believe that Jesus Christ is Immanuel, "God with us," and the Light of the World. As disciples of Jesus, we must bring His light to the world.

During Advent we prepare ourselves to bring the good news of Jesus to the poor. We try even harder to help care for the sick. We try to do what we can to stop injustice, discrimination, and oppression of any kind. We remember to be peacemakers.

COMING TO FAITH

Tell what you think Isaiah meant when he said our Savior would be:

- Immanuel
- a wise and just ruler
- a light shining in darkness
- one sent to bring good news

Maybe your group would like to bring in gifts of canned food or games for the children of your parish who are in need. Plan what you will do and make it a part of your Advent celebration.

89

Practicing Faith

An Advent Celebration

All sing:

O come, O come, Emmanuel,
And ransom captive Israel
That mourns in lonely exile here
Until the Son of God appear.
Rejoice! Rejoice, O Israel,
To you shall come Emmanuel!

Reading: (From Isaiah 61:1,3)

I am filled with the Lord's spirit.
God has chosen me and sent me
To bring good news to the poor,
To heal the broken-hearted,
To announce release to captives
And freedom to those in prison...
To give those who mourn
Joy and gladness instead of grief.

Leader: Let's pause now and think about these words of Isaiah. How can we bring Jesus' good news to the poor? healing to the broken-hearted? How can we bring freedom to those held captive by sin? How can we bring God's joy to others? (Silent reflection)

Leader: Jesus, we believe that You are Immanuel, God with us, our promised Savior.

All: Help us to live as Your disciples in the world today.

Leader: Jesus, You are the Light of the World.

All: Help us to live as Your disciples in the world today.

Leader: Jesus, You are the one sent by God to announce the good news.

All: Help us to live as Your disciples in the world today.

Leader: Jesus, You are the Son of God.

All: Help us to live as Your disciples in the world today.

Leader: Jesus, You are the Savior, who has come to free us. Help us to bring good news to the poor, to heal the broken-hearted, and to bring freedom to all.

Presentation of Gifts

Walking in procession, all carry gifts for needy children and place them on a prayer table or near an Advent wreath.

All stand and sing:

O come now Wisdom from on high
Who orders all things mightily,
To us the path of knowledge show
And teach us in Your ways to go.
Rejoice! Rejoice! O Israel
To you shall come Emmanuel!

Talk with your catechist about ways you and your family might use the "Faith Alive" pages. You might make the Angelus your family prayer for Advent. See page 205.

FAITH ALIVE AT HOME AND IN THE PARISH

This Advent lesson introduced the Old Testament prophecies that promised the Savior, the Messiah—the one who would be a wise and just ruler, a light shining in the darkness, the bringer of good news, Immanuel (which means "God with us"). These are the great messianic prophecies fulfilled in Jesus.

Advent is a season to prepare again for the coming of God's Son into the world and into our lives, and His future coming in glory. It is a time to reflect on our Savior, who gives hope to the poor, heals the sick, and liberates the oppressed. As a family, ask yourselves: how can we share the spirit of Advent with those in need in our parish or elsewhere?

† Family Prayer from the Angelus

The angel of the Lord declared to Mary,
and she conceived by the Holy Spirit.
Hail Mary....

Behold the handmaid of the Lord,
be it done to me according to your word.
Hail Mary....

And the Word was made flesh
and dwelled among us.
Hail Mary....

(See page 205 for the complete prayer.)

Learn by heart Faith Summary

● The prophet Isaiah foretold the coming of the Savior as One who would be Immanuel—"God with us."

● Years later the angel Gabriel was sent to Mary to ask her to be the mother of the Savior.

● During Advent we prepare for Christmas by trying to serve the needs of others.

Random Acts of Kindness

On slips of paper have family members write ideas for "random acts of kindness" that can be done for one another and for others outside the family. Talk this over with your family. Collect their suggestions and write them below before putting them on slips. Then each one chooses a slip each week and tries to do what is suggested.

_____

_____

Review

Go over the *Faith Summary* together and encourage your fifth grader to learn it by heart, especially the third point. Then have him or her do the *Review*. The answers to numbers 1–4 appear on page 216. The response to number 5 will show your child's deepening understanding of Advent.

Fill in the blanks.

1. The prophet Isaiah said the Messiah would be called _____, which means "God with us."

2. God sent the angel Gabriel to ask Mary to be the _____.

3. Isaiah compared the coming of the Savior to the breaking forth of _____ in darkness.

4. Isaiah said the Savior would be a _____ ruler.

5. Tell one important way you can, as a follower of Jesus, be a "light" for the world.

_____

_____

_____

_____

_____

FAMILY SCRIPTURE MOMENT

Gather and have each person name or describe someone in whom they have "seen Jesus" (or some quality of Jesus). Then **Listen** to an Advent messenger.

The Jewish authorities sent some priests and Levites to John the Baptist to ask him, "Who are you?" John answered, "I am not the Messiah." Then he quoted the prophet Isaiah: "I am the voice of someone shouting in the desert: Make a straight path for the Lord!" The next day John saw Jesus coming to him, and said, "There is the Lamb of God, who takes away the sin of the world! I did not know who He would be, but I came baptizing with water in order to make Him known to the people of Israel."
From John 1:19–20, 23, 29, 31

Share how each one can point others to Jesus.

Consider for family enrichment:

■ By his fasting and prayer, John the Baptist prepared himself to recognize and proclaim the Messiah to the world.

■ By our Advent prayer and ministry, we make a path for the Lord in our lives. We look forward to the celebration of Christmas and to the second coming of Christ at the end of time.

Reflect and **Decide** What will we do as a family to be Advent messengers?

14 Celebrating Christmas

O come let us adore Him, Christ the Lord!

Our Life

In some Latin American countries the people celebrate a lovely Christmas custom called *Las Posadas* ("the dwellings"). Two children take the parts of Mary and Joseph as they look for a place to stay in Bethlehem. All the other children escort them as they go from house to house in the neighborhood. At each door all sing a carol. Then Mary and Joseph ask for a room. They are turned away until they come to the last house. Here they are welcomed in, and all join in singing a joyful carol. A party usually follows!

Does your family have any special Christmas customs? Tell about them.

Share what Christmas means to you.

Sharing Life

Share what you know about Christmas customs in other countries. Why do you think people celebrate Christmas in different ways?

Discuss: what is the most important thing to remember in our Christmas celebrations?

OUR CATHOLIC FAITH

Newborn Savior of All People

On Christmas Day, we celebrate the birth of Jesus. We remember that the Son of God became one of us and was named Jesus, because He is our Savior. Jesus brings God's life and love to all people.

Here is what we read in the gospel about Jesus receiving His name.

Before Jesus was born, an angel appeared to Joseph in a dream. The angel told him, "Mary will have a Son and you will name Him Jesus—because He will save His people from their sins."

From Matthew 1:18–22

The name Jesus means "God saves."

A week after Jesus' birth, Joseph, His foster father, followed the Jewish custom and named the newborn Savior Jesus.

Later the Holy Family went to the Temple in Jerusalem to present Jesus to God. A man named Simeon, who had been praying for the Promised Savior, took Jesus in his arms. Praising God, Simeon said, "Now, O God, You have kept Your promise. I have seen Your salvation...a light to reveal Your will to all people."

From Luke 2:21–32

People of many different languages, customs, and races celebrate the birth of Jesus because He is the Savior of all people. When we celebrate Christmas, we remember that Jesus Christ has united us to God and to people all over the world.

Celebrating the Birth of Jesus

During the first years of Christianity, pagans in Rome celebrated a feast of the sun on December 25. Our Church may have chosen that same day on which to celebrate Jesus' birth because we believe that Jesus is the true Light of the World.

Today Christians around the world celebrate Christmas in many different ways. All our Christmas preparations, customs, and decorations should help us to remember the meaning of Christmas.

The lights on our Christmas trees and in our windows remind us of Christ, the Light of the World. The Christmas tree, which is usually an evergreen tree, reminds us that Jesus brought us life that lasts forever. The Christmas cards and gifts that we give remind us that God shared God's own life and love with us.

During the Christmas season, we celebrate that God loved us so much that God's only Son became one of us. We celebrate Christmas best by sharing God's love with others.

COMING TO FAITH

Tell the story of Jesus' name.

Then have a *Las Posadas* procession. Choose someone to be Mary and someone to be Joseph. Go from group to group in your parish center asking for a room and singing carols like "O Come All Ye Faithful" and "Away in a Manger." Let the last "house" be the place where your group meets. Some of you can be the "hosts" who welcome Mary and Joseph. When all are gathered, share the prayer service.

Practicing Faith

Mary and Joseph kneel beside an empty crib. All the rest gather around them and sing:

O little town of Bethlehem
How still we see thee lie.
Above thy deep and dreamless sleep
The silent stars go by.
Yet in thy dark streets shineth
The everlasting light—
The hopes and fears of all the years
Are met in thee tonight!

Reader 1: While Mary and Joseph were in Bethlehem, the time came for Mary to have her baby. She gave birth to a son, wrapped Him in cloths and laid Him in a manger because there was no room for them in the inn.

(Someone places a wrapped doll or an image of the baby in the manger.)

Reader 2: There were shepherds in the area, living in the fields and keeping watch over their flock. An angel of the Lord appeared to them and the glory of the Lord shone around them, and they were very much afraid. The angel said to them:

Angel: You have nothing to fear. I come to proclaim good news to you to be shared by all the people. This day a Savior has been born to you. Let this be a sign to you: in a manger you will find an infant wrapped in swaddling clothes.

Angels: Glory to God in high heaven, peace on earth to those on whom God's favor rests!

Shepherds: Let us go over to Bethlehem and see this event that has come to pass, which the Lord has made known to us!

Reader 3: The shepherds went with haste and found Mary and Joseph—and the baby lying in the manger.

From Luke 2:6–16

All sing "Silent Night"
(in Spanish, if possible):

Noche de paz, noche de amor.
Todo duerme en derredor.
Entre los astros que esparcen su luz,
Bella anunciando al niñito Jesús
brilla la estrella de paz,
brilla la estrella de paz.

Talk with your catechist about ways you and your family might use the "Faith Alive" pages. Ask family members to help create prayers for the tree, the lights, the star.

FAITH ALIVE AT HOME AND IN THE PARISH

In this lesson your son or daughter was reminded that the name Jesus means "God saves." Jesus came to be our Savior and His saving grace is for all people. All Christians celebrate Christmas and, though customs differ in different parts of the world, we all rejoice in the truth that God loved us so much that God's Son came to dwell among us and to be like us in all things, except sin.

Talk together as a family about your Christmas customs that recall the true meaning of Christmas—the lights that remind us that Christ is the light of the world; the Christmas tree, an evergreen, that reminds us of life that lasts forever; the Christmas crib that reminds us that Christ came to us in poverty and peace. If you have special Christmas customs from your own childhood, be sure to share them with your children. Explore parish customs as well, and how you plan to be a part of parish events on a continuing basis.

† Family Prayer

Jesus, help us to follow the star
And find the place where now You are—
No longer lying in manger bed,
But in our human hearts instead.

Learn by heart Faith Summary

- The name Jesus means "God saves."
- Jesus is the Light of the World.
- Jesus came to bring us everlasting life.

Make up a short prayer to say with your family as you:

- put up your Christmas tree (everlasting life).
- put lights in your window (Light of the World).
- put the star on your tree (finding Christ).

_____

_____

_____

_____

_____

Review

Go over the *Faith Summary* together and encourage your fifth grader to learn it by heart, especially the first statement. Then complete the *Review*. The answers to numbers 1–4 appear on page 216. The response to number 5 will show how well your child understands the deeper meaning of Christmas.

Circle **T** (True) or **F** (False).

1. The name *Jesus* means "Immanuel."   **T   F**

2. Simeon had been praying for the promised Savior.   **T   F**

3. All Christians celebrate Christmas the same way.   **T   F**

4. Jesus Christ came to unite all people to God.   **T   F**

5. How do you think Jesus wants us to celebrate Christmas?

_____

_____

_____

_____

_____

_____

FAMILY SCRIPTURE MOMENT

Gather and if possible, light a large candle. Then **Listen** to the true meaning of Christmas.

Before the world was created, the Word already existed; He was with God, and He was the same as God. From the very beginning the Word was with God. Through Him God made all things. The Word was the source of life, and this life brought light to humankind. The light shines in the darkness, and the darkness has never put it out. The Word became flesh and, full of grace and truth, lived among us. We saw His glory, the glory which He received as the Father's only Son.
From John 1:1–5, 14

Share Ask: What images of Jesus do we hear in this passage? What do people think "the Word became flesh" means for us?

Consider for family enrichment:

■ In these opening words of John's Gospel, Jesus is proclaimed as the eternal living Word, who reveals God to us.

■ At Christmas we welcome Jesus as the Word made flesh, who makes His home in us.

Reflect As disciples of Jesus Christ, how might we reveal the glory of God's only Son in our daily lives?

Decide How will our family welcome the Word among us this Christmas?

SUMMARY 1 ▪ REVIEW

Lesson 1—Jesus Christ Reveals God

- Jesus Christ is both human and divine.
- Jesus showed us that "God is love" by the things He said and did.
- God works through us and others to show God's love in the world.

Lesson 2—Jesus Christ and the Kingdom of God

- Jesus announced the good news of the kingdom, or reign, of God. The good news is that God loves us and will always love us.
- The reign of God is the power of God's life and love in the world.
- Jesus lived His whole life for the reign of God and calls us to do the same.

Lesson 3—Jesus Christ Blesses Our Lives

- Jesus invited everyone to live for the reign of God.
- Forgiveness heals the separation from God and from others that sin causes.
- Like Jesus, we try to forgive those who hurt us, no matter how great the hurt.

Lesson 4—The Church Carries on Jesus' Mission

- The Holy Spirit helps the Church carry on the mission of Jesus to all people.
- Jesus is the head of the Church, His body, and we are its members.
- Like Jesus, the Church serves people and brings them Jesus' healing and forgiveness.

Lesson 5—The Sacraments and the Church

- A sacrament is an effective sign through which Jesus Christ shares God's life and love with us.
- There are seven sacraments: Baptism, Confirmation, Eucharist, Reconciliation, Anointing of the Sick, Matrimony, and Holy Orders.
- We receive God's grace in the sacraments.

SUMMARY 1 · REVIEW

Lesson 8—Jesus Christ Brings Us Life (Baptism)

- We receive new life at Baptism when we are reborn of water and the Holy Spirit.
- At Baptism we are initiated into, or begin to become members of, the Church, the body of Christ.
- Our Baptism calls us to live for the reign of God.

Lesson 9—Jesus Christ Strengthens Us (Confirmation)

- Confirmation is the sacrament in which we are sealed with the Gift of the Holy Spirit and strengthened to give witness to the good news of Jesus Christ.
- In Confirmation the Holy Spirit fills us with the gifts that we need to live our Christian faith.
- We live our Confirmation when we become witnesses to the reign of God in the world.

Lesson 10—Jesus Christ Feeds Us (Eucharist)

- The Eucharist is the sacrament of the Body and Blood of Christ.
- Jesus is the Bread of Life. The food that Jesus gives us is His own Body and Blood.
- We respond to the gift of the Eucharist by living for the reign of God.

Lesson 11—Our Church Celebrates the Eucharist (The Mass)

- The two major parts of the Mass are the Liturgy of the Word and the Liturgy of the Eucharist.
- During the Liturgy of the Word, we listen to God's word from the Bible.
- During the Liturgy of the Eucharist, our gifts of bread and wine become the Body and Blood of Christ.

Lesson 12—The Church Remembers (The Liturgical Year)

- The liturgical seasons of the Church year are Advent, Christmas, Lent, the Easter Triduum, Easter, and Ordinary Time.
- During the liturgical year we also honor and pray to Mary and the other saints.
- The liturgical year reminds us that we always live in the presence of God.

SUMMARY 1 ▪ TEST

Circle the correct answers.

1. Jesus is like us in every way except

   a. that He never laughed.

   b. that He never got angry.

   c. that He never sinned.

   d. that He never died.

2. We say that Jesus is divine because

   a. He is the Son of God.

   b. He is loving.

   c. He is kind and merciful.

   d. He is Mary's son.

3. Jesus showed us how to live for the reign of God by

   a. building church buildings.

   b. becoming Catholic.

   c. living the Law of Love.

   d. writing the Gospels.

4. The sacraments of initiation are

   a. Matrimony and Holy Orders.

   b. Baptism, Confirmation, and Eucharist.

   c. Reconciliation and Anointing of the Sick.

   d. Eucharist and Holy Orders.

5. Sacraments are

   a. powerful signs of Jesus' presence with us.

   b. celebrations of our Church.

   c. sources of God's grace.

   d. all of these

Complete the following sentences.

service   initiation   Holy Spirit
healing   Body and Blood

6. Baptism, Confirmation, and the Eucharist are called sacraments of

_____.

7. Reconciliation and the Anointing of the Sick are called sacraments of

_____.

8. Matrimony and Holy Orders are called sacraments of

_____.

9. In Baptism we are reborn of water and the

_____.

10. In the Eucharist ordinary bread and wine become the _____ of Jesus.

Think and decide:

Choose one of the sacraments. Write one way you will live that sacrament.

_____

_____

_____

_____

SUMMARY 1 ▪ TEST

Read the following sentences. Cross out the terms that are incorrect.

11. In Baptism we receive the help of (the Holy Spirit/holy water) to live our new life of grace.

12. In Confirmation the Holy Spirit gives us gifts that help us live and witness (our faith/our citizenship).

13. The (Blessed Sacrament/holy oil) is kept in the tabernacle.

14. The Fruits of the Holy Spirit are signs that we (are living/need help to live) as witnesses to our faith.

15. The food that Jesus gives us as our Bread of Life is (ordinary bread and wine/Jesus' own Body and Blood).

16. We honor Mary on December 8, the feast of (the Immaculate Conception/the Ascension).

17. Jesus first gave us the gift of His Body and Blood at (His ascension into heaven/the Last Supper).

18. During the liturgical season of (Christmas/Lent) we prepare for Easter.

19. The Easter Triduum begins on (Ash Wednesday/Holy Thursday).

20. The Church remembers and celebrates the resurrection of Jesus on (Good Friday/ Easter Sunday).

Think and decide:

We have learned about many feasts of the Church's liturgical year. Choose one feast. Tell how you will celebrate it and how it helps you to live your Baptism.

Feast _____

_____

_____

_____

I will celebrate the feast by

_____

_____

_____

_____

I will live my Baptism by

_____

_____

_____

_____

Name _____

Your son or daughter has just completed Unit 2. Have him or her bring this paper to the catechist. It will help you and the catechist know better how to help your fifth grader grow in faith.

_____ He or she needs help with the part of the Summary/Review I have underlined.

_____ He or she understands what has been taught in this unit.

_____ I would like to speak with you. My phone number is _____.

Signature: _____

15 Jesus Christ Forgives Us
(Reconciliation)

Jesus, forgive us
our trespasses
as we forgive
those who
trespass
against us.

OUR LIFE

John Newton was a Scottish sea captain in the middle of the 19th century. He became very prosperous because of the cargo he carried—human cargo. Newton was a slave trader. He took people from Africa and sold them to slave traders in the new world.
He did this for some years.
Then something happened to change him.
Later he called it "grace."

Newton took a close look at his life and saw clearly the evil he was doing. He left the sea and the slave trade and spent his days in prayer asking God's mercy. As time went by he experienced great peace; he knew that he was forgiven. Newton tried to express in words the amazing grace of God's forgiving love. What he wrote has become one of the most loved Christian hymns in the world.

> Amazing grace, how sweet the sound
> That saved a wretch like me.
> I once was lost, but now am found;
> Was blind, but now I see.

What two "amazing" things did God's grace do for Newton?
Tell how you feel when you are forgiven.

SHARING LIFE

Discuss with one another what it means to be truly forgiven. Begin by saying, "True forgiveness means . . . ."

What part do you think forgiveness should play in the life of a Christian? in a family? in a parish?

Reconciliation, A Sacrament of Healing

Jesus announced the good news that God always forgives our sins when we are sorry for them.

We sin when we freely choose to do what we know is wrong. We disobey God's law on purpose. When we sin, we fail to live as we should as members of the Church and disciples of Jesus.

The Catholic Church teaches us that we can sin in thought, in word, or in action. Some sins are so serious that by doing them we turn completely away from God's love. We call them mortal sins.

A sin is mortal when:

● what we do is very seriously wrong;

● we know that it is wrong and that God forbids it;

● we freely choose to do it.

Other sins are less serious. These are called venial sins. By them we do not turn away completely from God's love. But they still cause hurt to other people, ourselves, and the Church.

All sins are personal sins. But whole groups of people can sin, too. We call this social sin. Social sin happens when groups of people choose not to do God's loving will. For example, members of a group commit social sin when they treat unfairly people who are poor or different from them.

Sin is never just between God and one person. Our sins always hurt someone else. We must try to heal the hurt we cause by our sin. We must do and say things that show we are truly sorry. We must try not to sin again.

Reconciliation, or Penance, is one of the two sacraments of healing. This sacrament is a powerful and effective sign through which Jesus shares with us God's mercy and forgiveness of our sins. We know we are united again, or reconciled, to God and to our Church community.

When we celebrate Reconciliation, we praise and worship God. In this sacrament we receive God's help to do God's loving will, to avoid all forms of sin, and to live as God's people. For this reason, we celebrate Reconciliation even when we are not guilty of serious sin. The chart on the next page tells us the different parts of the sacrament of Reconciliation.

We can celebrate Reconciliation individually or communally. These ways, or rites, of celebrating Reconciliation are given in the chart on page 107. In both rites, we meet with a priest privately. By the power of the

Holy Spirit, the priest acts in the name of Christ and the Church to forgive sins in God's name.

We thank God for Reconciliation in our everyday lives. We try to bring God's peace to our families, our school, and our parish community.

FAITH WORD

Sin is freely choosing to do what we know is wrong. When we sin, we disobey God's law on purpose.

Sacrament of Reconciliation

Examination of Conscience: We ask the Holy Spirit to help us think about how well we are doing God's loving will.

Contrition: We say an Act of Contrition to tell God that we are sorry for our sins. We promise to try harder to avoid sin and to love others as God loves us.

Confession: We confess our sins to God by telling them to the priest in private. We make sure that we confess all mortal sins to the priest. He advises us how to live each day for the reign of God as Jesus wants. The priest will never tell anyone what he heard in confession.

Penance: Our penance can be a prayer or a good deed that helps make up for the hurt caused by our sins. We do the penance the priest gives us to show God that we are sorry and want to change. Doing our penance helps us to avoid sin and grow closer to God.

Absolution: By the power of the Holy Spirit, the priest gives us God's forgiveness, or absolution. He makes the sign of the cross over us and says in part, "Through the ministry of the Church may God give you pardon and peace, and I absolve you from your sins in the name of the Father, and of the Son,✝ and of the Holy Spirit."
We respond, "Amen."

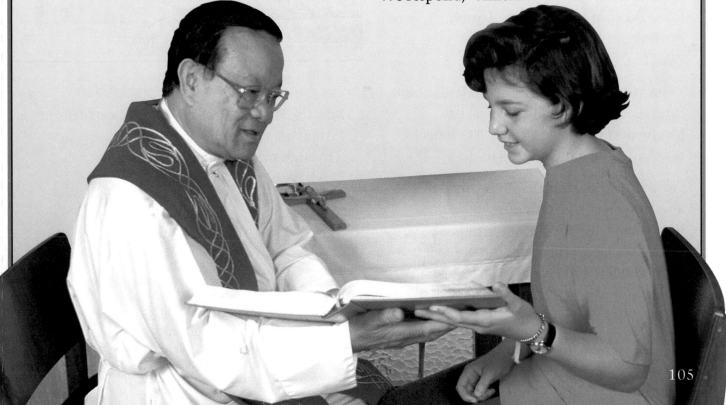

COMING TO FAITH

Challenge one another's knowledge of the key ideas of Reconciliation. Choose a card. Ask a group member to explain the term on the card. Check the answer by reading the definition on the back of the card. Key words are: conscience, contrition, Reconciliation, absolution, penance, confession.

PRACTICING FAITH

Gather in a circle. Sing "Amazing Grace."

Reader: God said, "Come back to Me. I will love you with all my heart...I am the source of all your blessings."
From Hosea 14:4,8

Reflection: Be very still. Talk to Jesus about forgiveness you need to receive, or forgiveness you need to give. Ask Jesus to help you do what you need to do.

Leader: To show our thanks for the amazing grace of God's mercy and forgiveness, let us offer one another a sign of God's peace. (Turn to those on your right and left and give a handshake of peace.)

Closing: All sing (or say) another verse of "Amazing Grace."
Through many dangers, toils, and snares
We have already come;
'Tis grace has brought us here thus far
And grace will lead us home.

Talk with your catechist about ways you and your family might use the "Faith Alive" pages. Invite a family member to celebrate Reconciliation with you.

FAITH ALIVE AT HOME AND IN THE PARISH

This chart will help your fifth grader celebrate the sacrament of Reconciliation either individually or communally. Go over both ways to make sure he or she understands each rite.

Individual Rite of Reconciliation

● Before entering the Reconciliation room, we examine our conscience.

● The priest welcomes us in the name of Jesus Christ and the Church. We make the sign of the cross together.

● We listen to a reading from the Bible.

● We confess our sins to God by telling them to the priest. The priest talks to us about our sins. He gives us a penance.

● We pray an Act of Contrition like the one on page 205.

● In the name of God and the Church, the priest says the words of absolution and makes the sign of the cross. We know that God has forgiven us. We answer, "Amen."

● The priest then tells us to go in peace.

● We make sure to do the penance the priest gave us.

Communal Rite of Reconciliation

● We gather as a community and sing a song. The priest greets us and we pray together for God's mercy.

● We listen to readings from the Bible. The priest or deacon gives a homily, reminding us of God's mercy and our need for forgiveness.

● We examine our conscience by thinking about our sins. We pray an Act of Contrition together. We may pray a litany or sing a song. We tell God that we are sorry and ask for forgiveness.

● We pray the Our Father

● We confess our sins to the priest individually. We receive our penance from the priest and he gives us absolution from our sins.

● We gather together after our individual confessions. We show our thanks to God by singing or praying.

● The priest blesses us and we leave in God's peace to do our penance and try to sin no more.

Learn by heart **Faith Summary**

● Reconciliation is the sacrament in which we are forgiven by God and the Church for our sins.

● Examination of conscience, contrition, confession, penance, and absolution are important steps in the celebration of Reconciliation.

● In Reconciliation we receive God's help to do God's loving will, to avoid sin, and to live as God's people.

Review

Go over the *Faith Summary* together and encourage your fifth grader to learn it by heart, especially the first statement. Then have him or her do the *Review*. The answers to numbers 1–4 appear on page 216. The response to number 5 will show how well your son or daughter understands that being sorry also means making up with those we may have hurt by our sins. When the *Review* is completed, go over it together.

1. Order from 1–5 the steps in the individual rite of sacrament of Reconciliation.

____ We confess our sins to the priest.

____ The priest gives us absolution.

____ We are welcomed in Jesus' name.

____ We pray an Act of Contrition.

____ The priest gives us a penance.

2. All sins are
  a. venial.
  b. personal.
  c. mortal.
  d. social.

3. Reconciliation is a sacrament of
  a. initiation.
  b. healing.
  c. service.
  d. witness.

4. If we totally reject God we commit
  a. venial sins.
  b. personal sins.
  c. mortal sins.
  d. social sins.

5. How can you try to heal the hurt caused by sin?

_____

_____

FAMILY SCRIPTURE MOMENT

Gather and ask each family member to recall an experience of being forgiven. How does receiving forgiveness change us? Then **Listen** closely to the first words that the risen Lord says to the disciples.

The disciples were gathered behind locked doors, because they were afraid of the Jewish authorities. Then Jesus came and stood among them. "Peace be with you," He said. Then He showed them His hands and His side. Jesus said, "As the Father sent Me, so I send you." Then He breathed on them and said, "Receive the Holy Spirit. If you forgive people's sins, they are forgiven; if you do not forgive them, they are not forgiven."

From John 20:19–23

Share how each person feels about these words from the risen Christ.

Consider for family enrichment:

■ The risen Christ gives His frightened disciples the gift of His peace and sends them forth as reconcilers of others.

■ Our Church celebrates this ministry of forgiveness in the sacrament of Reconciliation, a sacrament of healing.

Reflect and **Decide** How might the Holy Spirit be calling us to "breathe" peace and forgiveness into other people's lives? What will be our response?

16 | Jesus Christ Helps Us in Sickness and Death
(Anointing of the Sick)

OUR LIFE

Ten-year-old Danny Cardo was dying. Leukemia was destroying his blood cells and without a bone marrow transplant his life would end in a matter of weeks. No one in his family was a close enough match to his bone marrow for a transplant—not even his twin sister. His family turned to God in prayer. His school friends and his whole parish joined in.

In California, far away from Danny's home in Vermont, a young woman named Clare had recently become a bone marrow donor. The computer linked her blood type with Danny's as a real match. The surgery was done "just in time," the doctor said.

Today Danny is a healthy, active eleven-year-old. He would like to meet Clare someday. "I thank God for my life," Danny says. "I would like to thank her, too."

Why do you think Danny's family and parish turned to God in prayer?

How do you think Danny felt to know so many people were praying for him?

What or who helps you when you are sick?

SHARING LIFE

Imagine you were Danny. How would it make you feel to be facing death?

What would you want your family and friends to do?

Discuss together the best way to handle serious illness.

Anointing of the Sick, A Sacrament of Healing

In His public ministry, Jesus showed great care and compassion for people who were sick. His most frequent miracles were those of healing. Jesus told His disciples to carry on this ministry of healing.

Jesus gave His Church the work of bringing God's healing power to the sick, the elderly, and the dying. By the power of the Holy Spirit, the Church carries on this mission of healing in the sacrament of the Anointing of the Sick.

Anointing of the Sick is one of the two sacraments of healing. This sacrament is a powerful and effective sign of Jesus' presence that brings strength and healing to the elderly, the sick, and the dying.

The celebration of this sacrament sometimes helps sick people to get well again. When that does not happen, the sacrament helps the sick face their illness with faith and trust. It also helps dying people to continue their journey to God in heaven.

Saint James writes in his New Testament letter that in this sacrament our sick bodies can be healed and our sins forgiven. He wrote:
"Is there anyone who is sick? Send for the Church elders who will pray for and rub oil on the sick person in the name of the Lord. This prayer made in faith will restore the person to health, and the sins the person has committed will be forgiven."
From James 5:14–15

The sacrament of Anointing of the Sick often takes place during a Mass after the Liturgy of the Word. Family, friends, and other members of the parish come together with the sick and elderly to pray for and support them.

Anointing of the Sick is also given at home and in the hospital to those who are very ill or dying. The picture on page 113 shows how to prepare for this sacrament.

The two most important signs of the sacrament are the laying on of hands and anointing with oil. The priest first lays his hands on the head of the sick or elderly person. This is a sign of God's blessing.

He then anoints the person's forehead with oil, saying,
"Through this holy anointing
may the Lord in his love
and mercy help you
with the grace of the Holy Spirit."

He then anoints the person's hands, saying, "May the Lord who frees you from sin save you and raise you up."

Every Catholic should understand how this sacrament is celebrated. When a Catholic is seriously ill, a priest should be notified. In this way we help our friends and relatives who are sick.

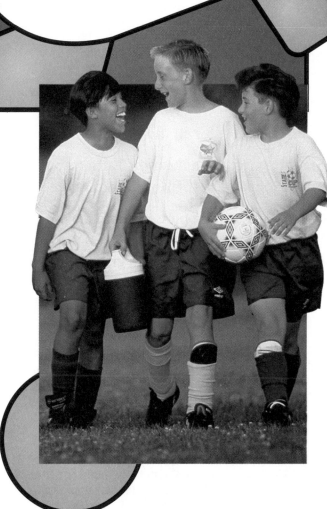

Living the Sacrament

God wants us to respect our bodies by taking care of them. Some sickness or disease cannot be avoided. Other illnesses can be avoided if we eat healthful foods, get enough sleep, and exercise properly.

Most importantly, we must not abuse or harm our bodies. Drinking alcohol to excess and using tobacco are dangerous and bad for our health.

No matter what our friends do or ask us to do, God will give us the courage to say no to illegal drugs. God will also help us to try again if we fail.

We can continue Jesus' mission of bringing God's healing power to all the world. We can respect our bodies. We can support our Church's efforts to eliminate disease, suffering, hunger, homelessness, and war in our world.

COMING TO FAITH

Act out a celebration of the sacrament of Anointing of the Sick.

Tell how we can live this sacrament in our daily lives.

PRACTICING FAITH

Ask your catechist about some people in your parish who are in need of your loving care.

Decide together some things that you, your friends, or your family will do to help these people.

†Praying for the Sick

Place in a bowl on a prayer table the names of people who are sick. Pray this blessing from the Bible for all these people.

Leader: In the name of the Father, and of the Son, and of the Holy Spirit. Amen.

All: May the Lord bless you and take care of you;
May the Lord be kind and gracious to you;
May the Lord look on you
with favor and give you peace.

From Numbers 6:24–26

Take turns praying for your special person by name.

Talk with your catechist about ways you and your family might use the "Faith Alive" pages. Ask your family to pray the prayer with you.

In this chapter your fifth grader has learned more about the sacrament of Anointing of the Sick. Many Catholics will recognize this sacrament by its former name, Extreme Unction. The change of name came from the renewal of the sacraments called for by the Second Vatican Council. Now the Church has returned to the early Christian understanding of this sacrament as one of healing, and not simply a sacrament limited to the dying. This is why the sacrament is called Anointing of the Sick.

In its faithfulness to the healing mission of Jesus, the Church invites the sick and dying to come to Him, seeking physical and spiritual health. The anointing of heads and hands with holy oil is a powerful sign of Jesus' loving presence to the one who is suffering.

When Holy Communion is given to a dying person, it is called Viaticum. Viaticum means "food for the journey."

Ask your fifth grader to tell your family about the Anointing of the Sick. Then let him or her use this drawing to show how your family should prepare for and celebrate this sacrament when it is needed by someone in your home.

† Family Prayer

God of compassion,
you take every family under your care
and know our physical and spiritual needs.
Transform our weakness by the strength
 of your grace
and confirm us in your covenant
so that we may grow in faith and love.
(From *Pastoral Care of the Sick*)

Learn by heart Faith Summary

● The sacrament of Anointing of the Sick brings God's special blessings to those who are sick, elderly, or dying.

● Anointing of the Sick is one of the two sacraments of healing.

● We must respect our bodies by caring for them. We must work to eliminate sickness and evil from the world.

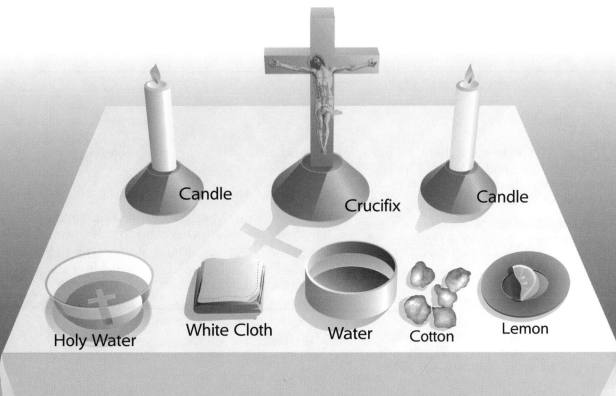

Candle

Crucifix

Candle

Holy Water

White Cloth

Water

Cotton

Lemon

Review

Go over the *Faith Summary* together and encourage your fifth grader to learn it by heart, especially the first statement. Then have him or her do the *Review*. The answers to numbers 1–4 appear on page 216. The response to number 5 will help you to see how well your fifth grader understands that one way we live this sacrament is by caring for our bodies. When the *Review* is completed, go over it together.

Circle the letter beside the correct answer.

1. Our Church cares for the sick, especially in the sacrament of
   a. Reconciliation.
   b. Anointing of the Sick.
   c. Baptism.
   d. Confirmation.

2. Anointing of the Sick can be celebrated
   a. during Mass.
   b. at home.
   c. in a hospital.
   d. all of the above

3. The two most important signs in Anointing of the Sick are
   a. laying on of hands and anointing.
   b. water and oil.
   c. the words and actions of absolution.
   d. bread and wine.

4. We live the sacrament of Anointing of the Sick when we
   a. ignore the homeless.
   b. take illegal drugs.
   c. respect our bodies.
   d. eat only "junk" foods.

5. Tell how you will respect your body.

_____

_____

_____

_____

FAMILY SCRIPTURE MOMENT

Gather and ask: How does our faith affect our hopes for someone who has died? Then **Listen** as Jesus visits a friend whose brother has just died.

When Martha heard that Jesus was coming, she went out to meet Him. Martha said to Jesus, "If You had been here, Lord, my brother would not have died! But I know that even now God will give You whatever You ask for." "Your brother will rise to life," Jesus told her. "I know," she replied, "that he will rise to life on the last day." Jesus said, "I am the resurrection and the life. Whoever believes in Me will live, even though he dies; and whoever lives and believes in Me will never die."

From John 11:20–26

Share what you heard in this reading for your life.

Consider for family enrichment:

■ Jesus invites Martha to express her faith in Him as "the resurrection and the life."

■ In the sacrament of Anointing of the Sick, the Catholic Church extends Jesus' healing love to the sick and dying.

Reflect How might we better minister to the sick and dying in our parish?

Decide How will we reach out to any who are sick or elderly in our family?

114

17 Jesus Christ Helps Us to Love

(Matrimony)

Loving God, help us to grow as people who understand and keep our promises.

OUR LIFE

Most fairy tales end with the prince and princess "living happily ever after." It is an ending we expect. Real life, however, can be very different. People who get married plan to live happily ever after, too.

The couples promise to stay together "until death us do part." But real life is full of good times and bad times, joys and sorrows, sickness and health.

How do couples make marriage work? Here are some responses from real people.

● "We try to love each other. That's what is most important."
(Jennifer and Steven, newlyweds)

● "We keep trying to grow and change together—we're partners in everything."
(Gilberto and Maria, married 10 years)

● "When we have problems, we work them out. Marriage takes *work*!"
(Roy and Linda, married 21 years)

● "We are best friends. We always will be."
(Jim and Tiana, married 46 years)

What do you think about what these couples are saying about marriage?

Then ask yourself: How well do I keep promises?

SHARING LIFE

Discuss together:

● things that make it difficult for couples to keep their promises

● things couples might do to help them keep their promises

Matrimony, A Sacrament of Service

Jesus calls all His disciples to love God, love others, and love themselves. The Church celebrates that call to love in a special way in the sacrament of Matrimony, or marriage.

Matrimony is one of the two sacraments of service. Married couples promise to serve each other with love and to serve the whole Church. They enter into a lifelong covenant of love. This is their vocation.

They serve the Church by their love and share in God's creation in a very special way when they give birth to children. Every married couple must be ready to welcome and raise lovingly the children God wishes them to have. In Matrimony God gives a man and woman the special grace and blessings to build a truly Christian family together.

In the sacrament of marriage, the Church brings God's love and blessing to the newly married couple. Their love is a sign of God's love in the world. Jesus Himself becomes a special partner in their relationship. Jesus wants to help every couple live out their marriage covenant.

The Holy Spirit gives the couple the grace to live this sacrament faithfully and well.

Catholics celebrate marriage as a sacrament. It is usually celebrated in the parish of the bride or groom. In the Catholic celebration of marriage, the couple themselves are the ministers of the sacrament. After the Liturgy

of the Word, the bride and groom stand before the priest or deacon, who witnesses the couple's promises for Christ's community, the Church.

Individually they vow to each other, "I, (Name), take you, (Name), to be my wife [or husband]. I promise to be true to you in good times and in bad, in sickness and in health. I will love you and honor you all the days of my life." These are called the marriage vows, or promises.

Jesus comes to the couple and unites them in love as Christ loves His Church. The Holy Spirit strengthens and blesses their love.

The sacrament of **Matrimony** is a powerful and effective sign of Christ's presence that joins a man and woman together for life.

Their married love becomes a sign of God's love for the world.

After they exchange their vows, the bride and groom usually give each other wedding rings as signs of their new union.

After the Our Father of the Mass, the priest or deacon gives the nuptial blessing. In this prayer, the Church asks God to help the couple love each other as Jesus loves us, share their love with their children, and raise them to be Jesus' disciples.

As another sign of their union, the bride and groom, if both are Catholics, may receive Holy Communion together. They ask Jesus to help them live their marriage promises with love all their lives.

Sometimes husbands and wives struggle in their marriages. But children are not to blame when their parents separate or divorce. Separation or divorce does not mean people are bad. This is a very difficult time for the whole family. No matter what happens,

God continues to love each person and always offers the help that is needed.

Learning to Love

Marriage is a long way off for us. We can prepare now for this sacrament by learning to love, respect and care for our family and friends in the same way that God always loves us.

We should learn to practice unselfish love. Parents often place their children's needs before their own. We can practice this kind of unselfish love now by doing things generously for our parents, for our brothers and sisters, and for our friends.

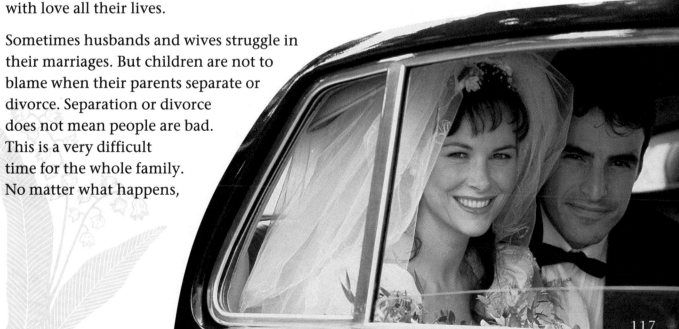

COMING TO FAITH

Reread the marriage vows on page 116. These are the promises the man and woman make to each other on their wedding day and forever. Describe in your own words what they are promising.

Why do you think the Church considers Matrimony a sacrament of service?

PRACTICING FAITH

† **Praying for Married Couples**

Praying for married couples is one of the most important ministries, or services, young people can offer.

Offer the following prayer together.

Leader 1: Jesus, You shared the joy and laughter of wedding celebrations.

All: Share Your joy with all married couples—especially those who are closest to us.

Leader 2: Jesus, You treated women and men equally.

All: Help wives and husbands to live together as equal partners and loving friends.

Leader 3: Jesus, You want marriage to last forever, like God's love for us.

All: Guide those whose marriages are in trouble. Help divorced or separated couples.

Leader 4: Jesus, help all Your disciples to follow Your command to love and to be faithful friends.

All: Amen.

Talk with your catechist about ways you and your family might share the "Faith Alive" pages together. Before doing the activity you might ask family members for their ideas.

Your fifth grader has learned more about the sacrament of Matrimony. Invite her or him to tell you what the sacrament means, and what young people can do now to learn to prepare for marriage if that is their vocation. The Second Vatican Council described marriage as a covenant of life and love.

Read the Bible story of the marriage feast at Cana from John 2:1–11. Talk about God's love for married couples and families. Also talk about the fact that God does not abandon families separated by death or divorce.

Decide and share what each of you will do this week to grow in unselfish love for and service to one another in your parish.

Do the activity below together to help your fifth grader grow in understanding what marriage really means.

† Family Prayer

May the Lord Jesus, who was a guest at the
    wedding in Cana,
bless my family and friends.

Learn by heart Faith Summary

● The sacrament of Matrimony is a powerful and effective sign of Christ's presence that joins a man and woman together for life.

● Married couples promise to serve each other and the whole Church. Matrimony is a sacrament of service.

● We can prepare now for Matrimony by trying to love others as God loves us.

Designing a Wedding Ring

Write what you would like printed inside a family member's wedding ring to remind him or her of the marriage covenant of love and service.

_____

_____

_____

_____

Review

Complete the following statements.

1. Matrimony is a sacrament of service. The best service Christians can give the world is

_____.

2. In the marriage vows a man and a woman promise to

_____.

3. Jesus Christ unites a husband and wife in love as Christ loves

_____.

4. Married love is a sign of _____.

5. How will you prepare now to be a good marriage partner someday?

_____

_____

_____

_____

FAMILY SCRIPTURE MOMENT

Gather and recall memories of a wedding in the extended family. Ask: For Catholic couples, what difference should their faith make to their marriage? Then **Listen** to a wedding story from John's Gospel.

There was a wedding in the town of Cana. When the wine had given out, Jesus' mother said to Him, "They are out of wine." Jesus said to the servants, "Fill these jars with water." They filled them, and then He told them, "Now draw some water out and take it to the man in charge." They took him the water, which now had turned into wine. He tasted it and said to the bridegroom, "You have kept the best wine until now!" Jesus performed this first miracle in Cana in Galilee; there He revealed His glory.
From John 2:1–3, 7–11

Share Imagine being at the wedding feast at Cana. Describe what you learn from the experience.

Consider for family enrichment:

■ In the Bible, a wedding feast often symbolizes the kingdom of God, in which love, peace and joy flow freely.

■ Catholics believe marriage is a sacrament and a sign of God's reign of love.

Reflect and **Decide** How might we turn the "water" of poverty or sorrow into the "wine" of gratitude or gladness for a married couple? For whom will we do this? When?

18 Jesus Christ Calls Us to Serve
(Holy Orders)

Loving God,
fill Your
Church with
the spirit of
courage, love,
and service.

OUR LIFE

In each of these pictures a priest is ministering, or offering some service, to his parish. Tell:
- how each priest is serving.
- what difference the priest may be making in the lives of the people served.

Name other ways by which priests minister to, or serve, their people.

SHARING LIFE

If you were a priest, what would you want to do for those you serve? Circle one of the priestly ministries listed below.

baptizer	confessor	teacher
preacher	leader	friend
Mass Celebrant and presider	spiritual guide	

Think of a priest who has served you or your family in this ministry. How did he help?

Discuss as a group what qualities are needed to be a good priest. Why?

Jesus Christ Gives us Leaders

From among the disciples, Jesus chose twelve special helpers, called apostles, to be the first leaders of His Church. He showed them that being a leader means being a servant, not one who is served.

Jesus told them, "If one of you wants to be great, you must be the servant of the rest. For even I did not come to be served; I came to serve and to give My life to redeem many people."

From Mark 10:35–45

The Church grew so rapidly that soon more helpers were needed. The apostles, with the help of the Christian community, chose others to continue their work of teaching and leading the Church in worship and service. The apostles laid their hands on them and prayed that they would be strengthened by the Holy Spirit.

In time these successors of the apostles were called bishops. The bishops ordained still others as priests to help them. Deacons also were chosen to make sure that the needs of the poor, the lonely, the widowed, and the orphaned were met. The leader of the apostles was Saint Peter. As bishop of Rome, the pope carries on the ministry of Saint Peter.

Today our bishops, priests, and deacons continue the mission of the apostles. Our pope is the leader of the whole Catholic Church. Bishops lead and serve our dioceses.

In our parish, priests help us to be a Christian community caring for one another. They lead us in celebrating the sacraments and teach us how to live Jesus'

good news. They serve the whole community and encourage us to use our gifts in service, too. Deacons have a special concern and ministry for the poor and those in need.

Holy Orders, A Sacrament of Service

Holy Orders is the sacrament through which the ordained ministry of bishops, priests, and deacons is conferred by the laying on of hands followed by the prayer of consecration.

Our ordained ministers serve the Catholic community in four ways:

- They preach and teach the good news of Jesus Christ.
- They lead us in celebrating the sacraments.
- They lead us in working together to build up the Christian community.
- They help us to serve the poor and all those in need.

Holy Orders is the sacrament that confers the ordained ministry of bishops, priests, and deacons.

Bishops, priests, and deacons are ordained in the sacrament of Holy Orders. The sacrament of Holy Orders is celebrated during Mass. Only a bishop can ordain another bishop, priest, or deacon.

In ordaining priests, the bishop lays his hands on the head of each candidate and prays silently. This is the most important sign of the sacrament of Holy Orders. Then the bishop prays a prayer of consecration, or the prayer that "makes holy."

Each candidate for the priesthood is also anointed with holy oil. This is a sign of his special sharing in Christ's own priesthood through the ordained ministry.

Each receives a paten and chalice. With these the priest leads the community in celebrating the Eucharist.

Bishops, priests, and deacons are our ordained ministers. Today our Church is much in need of loving and caring priests. We need to ask the Holy Spirit to give those called to the ordained priesthood the strength to accept and live this vocation.

By Baptism each of us is given a share in the priesthood of Jesus Christ. We are not ordained ministers. But we, too, are called to share the good news of Jesus Christ and carry on His mission.

123

COMING TO FAITH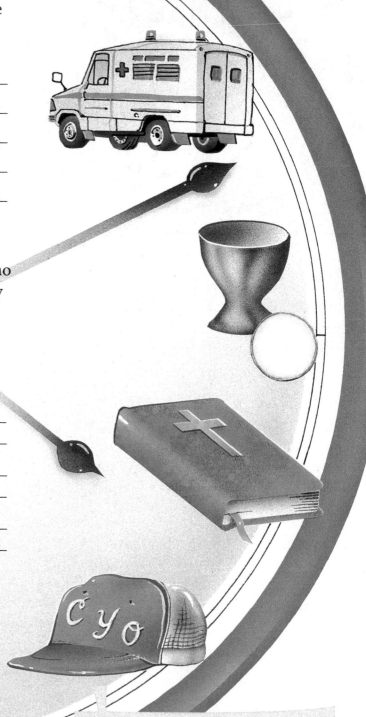

12

Work together and imagine a day in the life of a priest. Make a list of all the ways he serves the community.

_____

_____

_____

_____

PRACTICING FAITH

Think about some people in your parish who may not have been touched by the ministry of a priest. Will you tell your priest about these people?

Name one way you will help the priest in your parish serve the people who are:

hungry _____

_____

elderly _____

_____

ignorant of their faith _____

Circle the one you will do this week.

†Now gather together. Each one extend hands in prayer and say: "Lord Jesus, You ask us to serve and not be served. We pray for our ordained ministers. May those called to the priesthood respond with generous hearts. Amen."

Talk with your catechist about ways you and your family might use the "Faith Alive" pages. Then pray the prayer with your catechist and friends.

FAITH ALIVE AT HOME AND IN THE PARISH

Talk to your fifth grader about ways each one of us experiences the sacrament of Holy Orders through the ministry of the priests and deacons in our parish.

Discuss ways your family can support the ordained ministers in your parish. For example:

■ pray for them, especially at Mass.

■ help them in one of your parish programs.

■ show appreciation for their service.

■ contribute your own talents to the ministry of the parish.

Now ask each member of the family to write down what she or he will do this week to support your parish priest.

Then do these activities together:

■ Create a poster showing how a priest you know serves.

■ As a family, write a thank-you note to the priest illustrated on your poster.

† Family Prayer

Father,

in your plan for our salvation you provide shepherds for your people.

Fill your Church with the spirit of courage and love.

Raise up worthy ministers for your altars and ardent but gentle servants of the gospel.

(From the Mass for Priestly Vocations)

Learn by heart Faith Summary

● Jesus chose the twelve apostles to lead our Church in teaching and worship.

● Bishops, priests, and deacons are ordained in the sacrament of Holy Orders.

● Our ordained ministers lead us in building up the Christian community.

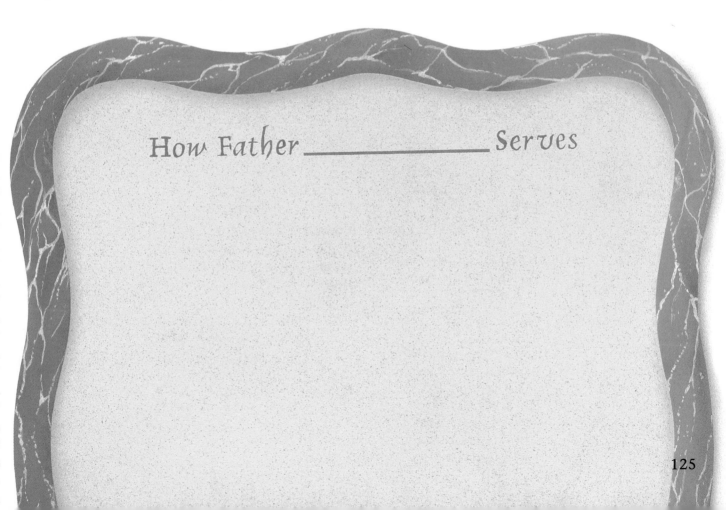

How Father _____ Serves

Review

Go over the *Faith Summary* together and encourage your fifth grader to learn it by heart. Then have him or her do the *Review*. The answers to numbers 1–4 appear on page 216. The response to number 5 will show how well your fifth grader understands our responsibility to help our priests. When the *Review* is completed, go over it together.

Complete the following sentences.

1. Jesus chose the twelve _____ to be the first leaders of our Church.

2. _____ are the successors of the apostles.

3. Those ordained ministers who have a special concern and ministry for the poor are called

   _____ .

4. The sacrament of Holy Orders is conferred through the _____ and the prayer of consecration.

5. Tell some ways you will support a priest who serves the people in your parish.

   _____

   _____

   _____

   _____

   _____

FAMILY SCRIPTURE MOMENT

Gather and ask: How do we know for sure that someone loves us? Then **Listen** as Jesus questions Peter.

After they had eaten, Jesus said to Simon Peter, "Simon, son of John, do you love Me more than these others do?" "Yes, Lord," he answered, "You know that I love You." Jesus said to him, "Take care of My lambs." A second time Jesus said to him, "Simon, son of John, do you love Me?" "Yes, Lord," he answered, "You know that I love You." Jesus said to him, "Take care of My sheep." A third time Jesus said, "Simon, son of John, do you love Me?" Peter said, "Lord, You know that I love You!"
From John 21:15–17

Share how you would respond to Jesus asking you this same question.

Consider for family enrichment:

■ Because Peter had denied knowing Jesus three times before the crucifixion, Jesus gave His chosen "Rock" three opportunities to express faithful love.

■ We honor and respect our pope as he carries on the ministry of Saint Peter today.

Reflect and **Decide** How might Jesus expect us to show support for our ordained ministers? How will we respond as a family in our parish?

Holy Spirit, help us to carry on the mission and ministry of Jesus.

Our Life

The parish council of St. Rose's Parish was upset to learn that so many young people between the ages of 18 and 30 and adults aged 30 to 45 seemed not to be active in the Church.

The council decided to invite these people back to the Church with a very special "Come Home for Easter!" celebration. Then they began to talk about who had the responsibility to organize the drive. This is what different members of the parish council said:

1. "Father Thomas is the priest and pastor. So he's the only one who can bring Catholics back to the Church. Of course, Sister Teresa and Mrs. Brown, the pastoral ministers, could help him."

2. "We're the people of the parish. Let's all work together with our ministers to build up our parish."

What answers do you think each of the following would give and why?

Your parish council You

Your parents Jesus

Sharing Life

Why do you think the Church needs priests, religious brothers and sisters, and lay pastoral ministers?

Discuss how Baptism calls all Christians to share in the ministry of Jesus.

What are some of the gifts that you can share with your parish community?

Sharing Christ's Priestly Mission

Before Jesus ascended into heaven, He said to His disciples, "Go, then, to all peoples everywhere and make them My disciples: baptize them in the name of the Father, the Son, and the Holy Spirit, and teach them to obey everything I have commanded you. And I will be with you always, until the end of the world."

From Matthew 28:19–20

Jesus wants His work to be carried on by all who are baptized. By Baptism all of us share in the great mission of Jesus to bring about the reign of God. This means that each of us has been called to live a holy life of service in our Church and our world.

This call is named our *Christian vocation*. Our Christian vocation begins at Baptism, the first sacrament of initiation. At Baptism we receive God's life of grace and are called to bring this life to others.

In Confirmation we are sealed with the Gift of the Holy Spirit and strengthened to live our Christian faith with courage.

In the Eucharist we are given the daily help we need to carry out our vocation as Christians.

Through Baptism every Christian shares in Jesus' priestly mission. We call this the *priesthood of the faithful*. This means that every baptized person has a vocation to live as Jesus lived. As disciples, we share in the priesthood of Jesus Christ.

The priesthood of the faithful is not the same as the ordained priesthood. Through the priesthood of the faithful, each one of us helps to carry on Jesus' mission in the world. Our pope and bishops have written special letters to all Catholics, reminding us of our responsibility to share the good news of Jesus. This responsibility is called evangelization. Every Christian has many opportunities to share his or her faith with others.

Carrying on Jesus' Mission

These are some of the vocations to which Jesus calls His people.

Married People: Jesus calls many women and men to the vocation of marriage and being parents.

Single People: Some people have a vocation to serve the Church as single, or non-married, men and women. By their daily words and actions, single people can show the world what it means to follow Jesus.

Ordained Ministers: Those who receive the sacrament of Holy Orders are called by Jesus to serve His Church as bishops, priests, and deacons. They share in Christ's priesthood in a special way.

Evangelization means spreading the good news of Jesus Christ and sharing our faith by our words and actions.

Religious: For many hundreds of years, men and women have joined religious communities as religious sisters, brothers, or priests. Religious serve our Church in parishes, hospitals, schools, and anywhere the good news needs to be preached. They make promises, or vows, of poverty, chastity, and obedience.

Laity: These are the single or married people in our Church. They serve our Church in many ways. Some dedicate years in serving as lay missionaries or as volunteers with religious communities in our country and around the world.

Pastoral Ministers: Pastoral ministers are religious brothers or sisters and lay people who have received special training to serve the needs of our Church. Some dedicate their entire lives to the tasks of parish leadership and education. Others serve by working with the poor and the homeless and for justice and peace.

Each of us has been called by Jesus to continue His mission of building up the reign of God on earth. All of us have a vocation to do something that only we can do.

COMING TO FAITH

Tell what a vocation is.
What is the Christian vocation of a baptized person?

List the talents and abilities God has given you. How can you use them to help others?

_____

_____

_____

_____

PRACTICING FAITH

Work together in your group to choose one of the following ways you will serve others this week.

● Offer to visit the sick with a eucharistic minister.

● Offer to help your catechist.

● Volunteer to work in a community project for the poor or the homeless.

● Volunteer as a tutor for younger or handicapped children.

● Other: _____

Write the plan for your project.
What will you do?
How and when will your group do it?
Who will lead the project?

† Loving God, help us to live our Christian vocation in following Jesus.

Talk with your catechist about ways you and your family might use the "Faith Alive" pages. Encourage family members to support you in what you and your group plan to do. Then pray the prayer for vocations with your catechist and friends.

FAITH ALIVE AT HOME AND IN THE PARISH

In this lesson your fifth grader has deepened his or her understanding that each of us has a particular vocation to build up the reign of God on earth. Ask your fifth grader to describe the different vocations presented in the lesson. It is not too early for fifth graders to consider what their special vocation might be. Encourage your fifth grader to pray and read about this vocation and to talk to those who follow it. Then discuss how she or he can prepare now for a life of service to others. Use this list to help you.

■ Celebrate the sacraments often so as to live each day better as a disciple of Jesus.

■ Pray each day that the Holy Spirit will guide you and give you courage to accept the vocation God has for you.

■ Read the Bible frequently.

■ Spend time trying to understand what is in this religion book so that you can explain it to others.

■ Listen carefully to the homilies at Mass and the faith stories told by your family.

■ Read the lives of your favorite saints.

† Family Prayer

Pray about a vocation you admire. Talk to those who follow this vocation. Say this prayer to help you know and follow your own vocation.

Holy Spirit, help me to know my special vocation in carrying on the mission of Jesus.

Learn by heart Faith Summary

● Jesus calls each of us to a specific vocation to carry on His priestly mission.

● Evangelization means spreading the good news of Jesus Christ and sharing our faith by our words and deeds.

● There are many vocations—married, ordained, religious, and single life. We are all called to carry on Jesus' mission.

Working for Justice and Peace

Select and write one way you will serve others by working for justice and peace.

_____

_____

_____

_____

Peace in the world starts with me.

Play by the rules.

Give of your time. Help the homeless.

131

Review

Go over the *Faith Summary* together and encourage your fifth grader to learn it by heart, especially the first two statements. Then have him or her go over the *Review*. The answers to numbers 1–4 appear on page 216. The response to number 5 will show how well your fifth grader understands the vocation we have right now through our Baptism to work for God's reign. When the *Review* is completed, go over it together.

1. Circle true (**T**) or false (**F**).

   We must be ordained in order to carry on Jesus' mission.   **T**   **F**

   The laity includes men and women who are single and married.   **T**   **F**

   All baptized Catholics are called to work for God's reign.   **T**   **F**

2. Our call to live a holy life of service is called our _____.

3. Our share in Jesus Christ's priestly mission is called _____.

4. Spreading the good news of Jesus by our words and deeds is called _____.

5. How will you work for God's reign right now?

   _____

   _____

   _____

   _____

FAMILY SCRIPTURE MOMENT

Gather and share what acts of service we do for one another in our family. **Listen** to a Last Supper story.

After Jesus had washed His apostles' feet, He put His outer garment back on. "Do you understand what I have just done to you?" He asked. "I, your Lord and Teacher, have just washed your feet. You, then, should wash one another's feet. I have set an example for you, so that you will do just what I have done for you. I am telling you the truth: no slave is greater than his master, and no messenger is greater than the one who sent him. Now that you know this truth, how happy you will be if you put it into practice!"

From John 13:12, 14–17

Share Imagine you are in this gospel scene. What would you learn from Jesus' washing of your feet?

Consider for family enrichment:

■ Jesus teaches His disciples the joy of service in ministry. The story of Jesus washing the feet of His disciples has become a treasured ritual during Holy Week.

■ We are called to be "foot washers" who are willing to serve others even in simple ways.

Reflect and **Decide** What feelings does this gospel passage arouse in us? How will we help one another to put Jesus' example into practice in our family? in our parish?

20 | Celebrating Lent

Jesus, help us to follow You this Lent so that we may live in Easter joy.

Our Life

A report tells us that during one year the average person in the United States eats about:

- 144 pounds of meat
- 81 pounds of vegetables
- 63 pounds of sugar
- 22 pounds of cheese
- 18 pounds of ice cream

It is also reported that during an average year people spend about:

- 26 billion dollars on television products
- 8.6 trillion dollars on clothes
- 20 billion quarters on video games

What do you think about this report?

Which of your possessions is the last you would give away? Why?

Sharing Life

Discuss with your group whether there are people who have:

- not enough food and things?
- just enough food and things?
- more than enough food and things?

Why are things the way they are, and what can be done about them?

Do you believe that Jesus wants us to share with others, especially the poor? Why or why not?

Jesus in the Desert

Before Jesus began to preach the good news of God's love to the people, He went into the desert to prepare Himself. After many days Jesus was very hungry, and the devil tempted Him, saying, "If You are God's Son, turn those stones into bread."

Jesus must have looked at the rocks around Him. Some of them may even have been shaped like loaves of bread. How easy it would have been to hold a rock in His hands and turn it into a hot, good-smelling loaf of bread.

But Jesus answered, "One cannot live on bread alone, but needs every word that God speaks."

The devil next took Jesus to Jerusalem. Setting Him on the highest point of the Temple, the devil said, "If You are God's Son, throw Yourself down. God will send angels to hold You up so that even Your feet will not be hurt."

Jesus answered, "The Scripture says, 'Do not put the Lord your God to the test.'"

The devil finally took Jesus to a very high mountain, and showing Him all the kingdoms of the world, said, "All this I will give You, if You kneel down and worship me."

Jesus answered, "Go away Satan! The Scripture says, 'Worship the Lord your God and serve only God.'"

Then the devil left Jesus.

From Matthew 4:1–11

After this, Jesus went out and began to preach the good news to all the people.

What do you learn from this story of Jesus being tempted?

A Time for Preparing

During the season of Lent we prepare for Easter. Lent helps us to understand the meaning of the death and resurrection of Jesus. We remember that in our Baptism we die to sin and rise to new life in Jesus. During Lent we try to prepare ourselves to live better the new life we received in Baptism. We also pray for those who are about to be baptized.

Sometimes we spend too much time eating, shopping, and playing games. We become so busy with our possessions that we can forget about God and others.

During Lent many Catholics give up snacks or eat less at meals. We help poor and hungry people. We spend more time with God by praying and reading from the Bible. These Lenten practices help us put God and people before our possessions.

During Lent we try more than ever to love God and others, as Jesus showed us, without expecting something in return.

We must prepare ourselves to carry on the mission of Jesus. We try to do this during Lent.

COMING TO FAITH

Here are some things we can do during the season of Lent.
Check off the thing that you will do to share in Jesus' mission.

_____ Spend more time reading the Bible
_____ Give away some toys or games
_____ Take part in Mass more often
_____ Forgive someone who has hurt me
_____ Be kind to someone who is ignored by others
_____ Give up one of my favorite foods
_____ Pray the stations of the cross
_____ Visit someone who is lonely
_____ Pray for the leaders of our Church

_____ Celebrate Reconciliation
_____ Pray with my family or friends
_____ Care for the environment
_____ Pray for those preparing for Baptism
_____ Bring food to the parish to give to a hungry family
_____ Work with people who are trying to make peace
_____ Reach out to someone who is being treated unfairly

Other things I can do:

_____

PRACTICING FAITH

A Prayer Service for Lent

✝ Gather in a circle.

Opening Hymn

"Come Back to Me" (Hosea)
or "Earthen Vessels"

Prayer

Leader: Jesus, we come together
to begin our preparation for Easter.
During the season of Lent, we
want to renew our desire to live
the way You taught us.

Gospel

Leader: A reading from the
holy gospel according to Mark.

(Read Mark 1:12–15)

Time for Reflection

Think about the Gospel reading. Read over
the list of Lenten practices you checked on
page 135. Now discuss together quietly what
your group might do together to join in
Jesus' mission this Lent.

Then pray the following prayer
together.

Jesus, during these forty days of Lent,
help us to follow You. Help us to live
more fully the new life we received in
Baptism. As Your disciples, we have
decided to do the following acts:

We will pray more by _____

_____

_____

We will act as peacemakers by _____

_____

_____

We will serve the poor and hungry by

_____

Closing Hymn

"Let There Be Peace on Earth"
or "Prayer of Saint Francis"

Talk with your catechist about ways you
and your family might use the "Faith
Alive" pages together. Share with family
members ways your family can pray,
fast, and give to the poor.

This lesson has explored more deeply the significance of the Lenten season in the life of a Christian. Your fifth grader has learned that Lent is a time to strengthen our hearts and wills against temptation as Jesus did when He prayed and fasted in the desert. Prayer, fasting, and almsgiving are traditional Lenten practices to help us renew the gift of faith that we first received in Baptism. Besides fasting on Ash Wednesday and Good Friday, Catholics also abstain from meat on these days and the other Fridays of Lent.

Your child has also learned that during Lent we join in prayer with those preparing for Baptism. We share our beliefs and give our support to people preparing for membership in our Church.

You might want to discuss with your family how you will deepen your own practice of prayer, fasting, and almsgiving this Lent.

Praying with the Bible

Prayers do not have to be long and wordy. The Bible often gives us short prayers that are very powerful. For example: "Lord, you know everything; you know that I love you!" (John 21:17)

Find other short prayers in your Bible, such as John 20:28, Luke 22:42, Psalm 23:1, Psalm 34:1, Isaiah 6:3.

Learn by heart Faith Summary

- Lent prepares us to enter more fully into the passion, death, and resurrection of Jesus.
- During Lent we try to love God and others without expecting something in return.

Write your favorite short prayer here.

Review

Go over the *Faith Summary* together and encourage your fifth grader to learn it by heart, especially the first statement. Then have him or her do the *Review*. The answers to numbers 1–4 appear on page 216. The response to number 5 will indicate your child's growing understanding of the Lenten challenge. When the *Review* is completed, go over it together.

Circle the letter beside the correct response.

1. Before Jesus began preaching He
   a. went into the desert.
   b. was tempted by Satan.
   c. fasted from food.
   d. all of the above

2. Satan tempted Jesus to
   a. eat stones.
   b. turn stones into bread.
   c. turn bread into stones.
   d. turn Satan into stone.

3. Satan tempted Jesus to
   a. worship him instead of God.
   b. leave him.
   c. fight with the angels.
   d. none of the above

4. We rise to new life in Jesus
   a. during Lent.
   b. in Baptism.
   c. in the desert.
   d. when we pray.

5. Tell one way you can put God and others before possessions.

_____

_____

_____

_____

FAMILY SCRIPTURE MOMENT

Gather and discuss what you think it means to live the truth. Then **Listen** to a Lenten story.

Pilate went back into the palace and called Jesus. "Are you the king of the Jews?" he asked Him. Jesus said, "My kingdom does not belong to this world; My followers would fight to keep Me from being handed over to the Jewish authorities." So Pilate asked Him, "Are you a king, then?" Jesus answered, "I was born and came into the world for this one purpose, to speak about the truth. Whoever belongs to the truth listens to Me."
From John 18:33, 36–37

Share why you associate Jesus with the truth and what it means to belong to the truth of Jesus.

Consider for family enrichment:

■ Although Pilate's question is intended as an insult, Jesus responds by telling the truth about His kingdom and identity.

■ By His example, Jesus teaches us to be truthful, courageous, and nonviolent in confronting sin or evil.

Reflect How can we show during Lent that we are people who "belong to the truth"?

Decide Pray together: Jesus, may we use each day of Lent as an opportunity to become more truthful, courageous, and nonviolent in opposing evil.

Alleluia! Jesus is risen and is still with us. Alleluia, alleluia!

OUR LIFE

It was a forgotten patch of earth almost lost among the dingy apartments. Full of weeds, garbage, and abandoned junk, it was just another piece of ugliness in this very tough part of the city. But not to Mr. Catelli. He had a dream. This plot of earth could live again. So one day Mr. Catelli went out and began to work.

Some neighbors saw what he was doing and offered to help. Soon the garbage was packed into bags and left for the sanitation trucks. Young people in the neighborhood started to drop by to help with the weeding. Soon

Mr. Catelli was laboriously turning the soil and adding loam. By now the whole neighborhood was involved, and Mr. Catelli had gifts of seeds, plants, and even trees. The planting began. "Now what?" the children asked. "Now we wait and water and let God work," Mr. Catelli answered.

Spring came and the lot was now a park full of flowers and grass and young trees. "Our park is beautiful!" everyone said. Mr. Catelli smiled. What was dead had come back to life.

What do you learn from this story of Mr. Catelli?

Name some things that give you new life.

SHARING LIFE

Have you ever helped something that seemed dead have new life? Tell about it.

Why are these experiences so full of surprise and joy?

Our Catholic Faith

Honoring Christ, Our Savior

The Sunday before Easter Sunday is called Passion, or Palm, Sunday. Passion Sunday is the first day of Holy Week. It prepares us for the Easter Triduum, the three days that begin on Holy Thursday evening and end with Evening Prayer on Easter Sunday.

On Passion Sunday we remember that Jesus and His friends went to the city of Jerusalem shortly before His arrest and crucifixion. The Gospel of Mark tells us the story as follows:

Jesus, riding on a donkey, came into the city of Jerusalem. As Jesus rode by, people spread their cloaks before Him on the road. Others cut branches off the trees and laid these on the road in front of Jesus. Others followed Jesus, shouting, "Praise God. God bless Him who comes in the name of the Lord. God bless the coming kingdom of King David. Praise be to God."

From Mark 11:1–11

Jesus came into the city of Jerusalem in triumph. He was honored and welcomed by the crowds. But within a few days, He would suffer, be crucified, and die.

On Passion Sunday, palm branches are blessed and given to us. We walk in procession into the church, singing and waving palm branches to honor Jesus.

The Easter Triduum

During the Easter Triduum we celebrate the paschal mystery. The word *paschal* means "passing over" or "passover." The paschal mystery is a remembering and celebrating of the events of Jesus' "passing" through suffering and death to new life in His resurrection.

On Holy Thursday evening we celebrate the Mass of the Lord's Supper. We remember that Jesus gave us the gift of Himself in the Eucharist.

On Good Friday in the Celebration of the Lord's Passion, we remember that Jesus was crowned with thorns, suffered, and died on the cross for our sins.

On Holy Saturday night we celebrate the Easter Vigil. We await the resurrection of Jesus and remember that we are baptized into His death and resurrection. On this night we welcome new members into the Church through the sacraments of initiation.

On Easter Sunday we celebrate the resurrection of Jesus and our new life in Christ. The Easter Triduum concludes with Evening Prayer on this day. Then all during the Easter season, we remember how Jesus Christ brought us the fullness of God's life and love.

COMING TO FAITH

Below is a list of some important celebrations of the Easter Triduum. Tell what we remember and celebrate during each. Write how you can take part in each celebration.

Evening Mass of the Lord's Supper

We celebrate ———————————
————————————————————
————————————————————

I can ————————————————
————————————————————
————————————————————

Celebration of the Lord's Passion
We celebrate ———————————
————————————————————
————————————————————

I can————————————————
————————————————————
————————————————————

Easter Vigil
We celebrate ———————————
————————————————————
————————————————————

I can ————————————————
————————————————————
————————————————————

Practicing Faith
An Easter Celebration

Opening Prayer

Leader: Jesus, we have prepared ourselves to share in the joy of Your resurrection. Open our hearts to receive Your new life.

An Easter Story

Group 1: Are You the only visitor in Jerusalem who does not know what things happened there to Jesus of Nazareth?

Group 2: What things?

Group 1: We had hoped that Jesus was the one who would set Israel free. But He was crucified. After His death, some women in our group went to the tomb and told us, "He is alive!"

Group 2: How slow to believe you are! Wasn't it necessary for the Messiah to suffer these things?

Narrator: Jesus explained many other things to them. As they came near the village toward which they were going, Jesus acted as if He were going on.

Group 1: Stay with us. It is getting dark.

Narrator: Jesus sat down to eat with them, took the bread, and said the blessing; then He broke the bread and gave it to them. Their eyes were opened and they recognized Jesus. Jesus then disappeared from their sight.

Renewal of Baptismal Promises

Leader: Do you reject Satan?

All: I do.

Leader: And all his works?

All: I do.

Leader: And all his empty promises?

All: I do.

Leader: Do you believe in God, the Father Almighty, creator of heaven and earth?

All: I do.

Leader: Do you believe in Jesus Christ, God's only Son, our Lord, who was born of the Virgin Mary, was crucified, died and was buried, rose from the dead, and is now seated at the right hand of the Father?

All: I do.

Leader: Do you believe in the Holy Spirit, the holy catholic Church, the communion of saints, the forgiveness of sins, the resurrection of the body, and life everlasting?

All: I do.

Blessing with Holy Water

All come to a prayer table on which a small bowl containing holy water has been placed. All bless themselves with the holy water by making the sign of the cross to remember the gift of new life given in Baptism.

FAITH ALIVE
AT HOME AND IN THE PARISH

This lesson is an immediate preparation for the Easter experience of moving with Jesus through death to new life. Your child was given a deeper understanding of the events of Palm Sunday and the Triduum—which begins with the Evening Mass of the Lord's Supper on Holy Thursday and ends Easter Sunday with Evening Prayer.

Easter is the greatest celebration of the Church year. It is a feast full of joy and triumph—the triumph in Jesus Christ of life over death. The resurrection of Jesus is the ultimate foundation of Christian faith.

If possible, have your family join with the parish in celebrating the Easter Triduum.

✝ Family Prayer

Lord of all hopefulness, Lord of all joy,
Whose trust ever childlike no cares
can destroy,
Be there at our waking and give us,
we pray,
Your Easter joy that forever will stay.

Learn by heart Faith Summary

● The paschal mystery celebrates the events of Jesus' "passing" through suffering and death to new life.

● On Holy Thursday we celebrate the gift of the Eucharist. On Good Friday we remember Jesus' suffering and death. On Easter we celebrate Jesus' resurrection.

We Are Easter People

Talk with your family about what it means when we say that Christians are "Easter" people. List all the ideas that are mentioned. Some might be: hope, joy, life, love. Perhaps you might make an Easter flag for your home using these ideas.

Review

Go over the *Faith Summary* together and encourage your fifth grader to learn it by heart. Then have him or her do the *Review*. The answers to numbers 1–4 appear on page 216. The response to number 5 will help you see how well your child understands the paschal mystery. When the *Review* is completed, go over it together.

Complete the sentences.

1. On Holy Thursday we celebrate _____.

2. On Good Friday we celebrate _____.

3. At the Easter Vigil and on Easter Sunday we celebrate _____

_____.

4. The above celebrations make up what is called the _____.

5. What do you think it means to be "baptized into Christ's death and resurrection"?

_____

_____

_____

_____

_____

_____

FAMILY SCRIPTURE MOMENT

Gather and recall the joy when loved ones have returned unexpectedly or paid surprise visits. Then **Listen** to an Easter story.

Mary Magdalene looked in the tomb and saw two angels there, sitting where the body of Jesus had been. "Woman, why are you crying?" they asked. She answered, "They have taken my Lord away, and I do not know where they have put Him!" Then she turned and saw Jesus standing there; but she did not know that it was Jesus. Jesus asked her, "Who is it that you are looking for?" She thought He was the gardener. Jesus said to her, "Mary!" She said in Hebrew, "Rabboni!" (This means "Teacher.") So Mary Magdalene went and told the disciples that she had seen the Lord.

From John 20:11–16, 18

Share Imagine you are at the tomb with Mary Magdalene. What are your feelings?

Consider for family enrichment:

■ In John's Gospel, Mary Magdalene is the first disciple to see and proclaim the risen Lord. Christ has a glorified body, which she, in her sorrow, does not recognize.

■ We rejoice with Mary in the risen Christ and go to share our faith with others.

Reflect and **Decide** How are we like Mary Magdalene? What will we do to proclaim the Easter message with others in our parish?

144

UNIT 3 ■ REVIEW

Jesus Christ Forgives Us (Reconciliation)

The Church celebrates all the sacraments by the power of the Holy Spirit. In the sacrament of Reconciliation Jesus Christ shares God's forgiveness of our sins. Reconciliation is one of the sacraments of healing.

Reconciliation, or Penance, may be celebrated individually or communally. In both rites, or forms of celebration, we confess our sins to a priest in private.

Examination of conscience, confession, contrition, penance, and absolution are important parts of Reconciliation.

Jesus Christ Helps Us in Sickness and Death (Anointing of the Sick)

In the sacrament of Anointing of the Sick, the Church carries on Jesus' mission of bringing God's healing power to the sick and dying. Anointing is one of the sacraments of healing. The two most important signs of this sacrament are the laying on of hands and anointing with oil.

We also carry on Jesus' mission of healing when we take care of and respect our bodies, and when we support our Church's efforts to eliminate disease and suffering in our world.

Jesus Christ Helps Us to Love (Matrimony)

Matrimony is a sacrament of service. It is a powerful sign of God's love and faithfulness. In Matrimony a bride and groom enter into a lifelong marriage covenant. They promise to love each other and serve the Church. We can prepare for Matrimony by being faithful in our friendships and practicing unselfish love.

Jesus Christ Calls Us to Serve (Holy Orders)

Jesus Christ chose twelve apostles to lead His Church. In time, the Church chose other leaders called bishops, priests, and deacons.

Holy Orders is a sacrament of service. Our bishops, priests, and deacons are ordained in the sacrament of Holy Orders to lead our Church in service and worship. The Pope is the leader of the whole Church. We support our ordained leaders by praying for them and helping them.

We Share Jesus Christ's Priesthood (Ministry)

Through Baptism every Christian shares in Jesus' priestly mission and ministry and is called to serve the Church. Each person has a vocation, or call, to serve others. There are many vocations: married, ordained, religious, and single persons. Our preparation for a life of service begins now.

UNIT 3 · TEST

Circle the correct answers.

1. The sign of receiving God's forgiveness in Reconciliation is the
   a. Act of Contrition.
   b. absolution.
   c. penance.
   d. examination of conscience.

2. The sacraments of healing are
   a. initiation and service.
   b. Anointing of the Sick, Baptism.
   c. Reconciliation, Anointing of the Sick.
   d. Confirmation, Eucharist.

3. The sacrament that brings God's healing to the sick, and dying is
   a. Holy Orders.
   b. Confirmation.
   c. Eucharist.
   d. Anointing of the Sick.

4. Through Baptism all Christians share in
   a. marriage.
   b. ordination.
   c. the priesthood of the faithful.
   d. confession.

5. Every baptized person has
   a. ordination.
   b. a vocation.
   c. vows.
   d. anointing.

6. The ministers of the sacrament of Matrimony are
   a. bishops.
   b. the bride and groom.
   c. deacons.
   d. priests.

7. The sacraments of service are
   a. Holy Orders and Matrimony.
   b. Baptism and Matrimony.
   c. Holy Orders and Confirmation.
   d. Eucharist and Reconciliation.

Answer the following questions.

8. Two ways to celebrate Reconciliation are

_____

_____

9. How does the Church continue Jesus' ministry of healing?

_____

_____

Think and decide:

What vocation do you think you will follow? Tell how you will prepare for it.

_____

_____

_____

Name _____

Your son or daughter has just completed Unit 3. Have him or her bring this paper to the catechist. It will help you and the catechist know better how to help your fifth grader grow in faith.

_____ He or she needs help with the part of the Review I have underlined.

_____ He or she understands what has been taught in this unit.

_____ I would like to speak with you. My phone number is _____.

146   Signature: _____

22 | Becoming a Catholic
(The Marks of the Church)

OUR LIFE

Groups such as youth organizations and sports teams have marks, or qualities, that clearly show what kind of a group each one is or would like to be. Choose one of the following situations and work with a partner to draw up your expectations, qualities, or "marks" for each one.

- You are putting together a "dream team" in any sport you wish.
- You are a musician and are assembling a band or an orchestra.
- You are organizing a youth service group.

What qualifications would you expect from individual members? from the group as a whole?

SHARING LIFE

We are members of the Church. Discuss together: What marks, or qualities, do you think the Church should have? Make a list.

Do you show that our Church has these qualities? How?

The Marks of the Church

The Church has four great identifying "marks," or qualities, that let people know the kind of community Jesus began. We say that the Church is one, holy, catholic, and apostolic. We must always keep trying to live these marks.

The Church Shows It Is One

Jesus wants all His disciples everywhere to be one with Him and with one another in the Holy Spirit.

When we say that the Church is one, we mean that all baptized persons are united in the body of Christ. We, though many, are made part of the one body of Jesus Christ through Baptism.

As Catholics we are united by the leadership of the pope and bishops. We celebrate our unity with Jesus and with one another in the Eucharist. We are united in faith and in love with Jesus Christ and one another.

But not all Christians share the same beliefs and practices. Over the centuries, some Christians became separated from the Catholic Church.

Today all Christians are called to pray and work for the full unity of the Church. Saint Paul once described the unity we should have: "There is one Lord, one faith, one Baptism; there is one God and Father of all, who is Lord of all, works through all, and is in all."

From Ephesians 4:5–6

The Church Shows It Is Holy

God alone is perfectly holy. The Church is holy because it is the body of Christ and because the Holy Spirit is present in the Church.

Jesus called His disciples to live holy lives, as He did. The holy lives of the apostles, the saints, and of all disciples of Jesus show the holiness of the Church.

God says to us, "Be holy, because I, your God, am holy" (from Leviticus 19:1–2).

We begin to share in God's holy life when we are baptized. The Church helps us to grow in holiness, especially through the sacraments.

We can show that the Church is holy by leading holy lives and by working for the reign of God in the world. We try to put God first in all we say and do. We try to live the Law of Love and work for justice and peace.

Today the Church continues to show it is catholic. Missionaries carry the good news to every country on earth. The Church works for the salvation of all people everywhere. We try to share our faith and welcome everyone to Jesus' community of disciples.

The Church Shows It Is Apostolic

When Saint Paul wrote to the early Christians, he reminded them that they were "built upon the foundation laid by the apostles" with the "cornerstone being Christ Jesus Himself" (Ephesians 2:20). The Church is apostolic, because it was founded on the apostles and tries to be faithful to the mission and beliefs Jesus gave them. The Church can trace itself back to the apostles.

Saint Peter led the first apostles as they carried on Jesus' mission. In the Catholic Church, Peter's successors are the popes. Today our Holy Father, the pope, carries on the work of Saint Peter. The other bishops carry on the work of the first apostles.

We can show that our Church is apostolic by learning all we can about our Catholic faith. We can pray for and help our missionaries. We can do our part in carrying out the mission Jesus gave to the first apostles.

Each time we pray the Nicene Creed at Mass, we say that we believe in the one, holy, catholic, and apostolic Church. Jesus asks each one of us to develop these marks, or qualities, in our own lives. In this way we show others that we are true disciples of Jesus Christ.

The Church Shows It Is Catholic

The word *catholic* means "universal" or "worldwide." The Church is to be a community in which all people of every race, color, nationality, and background are welcome. All are to hear the good news of Jesus Christ.

Jesus invited everyone to belong to His community and to follow Him. He commanded His disciples to be just as welcoming and to include everyone in carrying on His mission.

Before His ascension into heaven, Jesus told His disciples, "Go throughout the whole world and preach the gospel to all people" (from Mark 16:15). The disciples carried out Jesus' command.

COMING TO FAITH

Tell the name of:
your diocese, bishop, parish, pastor.

Now imagine that your bishop has asked your group to make a short TV spot showing how your diocese or parish tries to live the marks of the Church today. Plan your ideas together. Use the marks of the Church as an outline. You may draw sketches, write a script, or act it out.

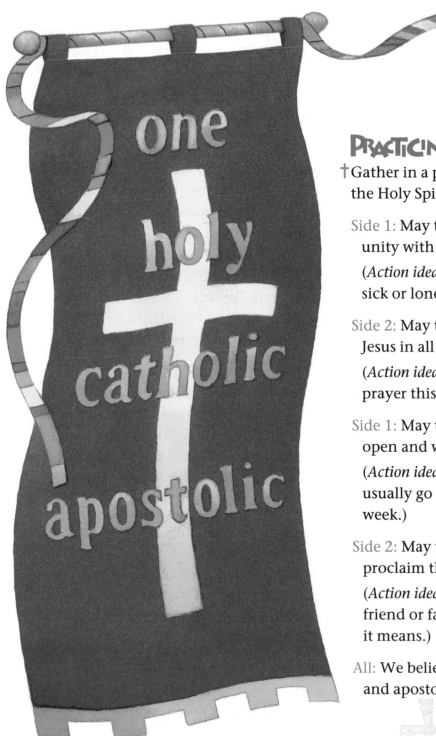

PRACTICING FAITH

†Gather in a prayer circle. Be very still and let the Holy Spirit guide us.

Side 1: May the Holy Spirit help us to live in unity with Jesus and one another.

(*Action idea*: Decide to help someone who is sick or lonely or poor this week.)

Side 2: May the Holy Spirit guide us to be like Jesus in all things.

(*Action idea*: Decide to set aside time for prayer this week.)

Side 1: May the Holy Spirit help us to be open and welcoming to all people.

(*Action idea*: Invite a friend, who does not usually go to Mass, to come with you this week.)

Side 2: May the Holy Spirit give us courage to proclaim the good news of Jesus.

(*Action idea*: Read a gospel story with a friend or family member. Talk about what it means.)

All: We believe in the one, holy, catholic, and apostolic Church. Amen.

Talk with your catechist about ways you and your family can use the "Faith Alive" pages. Ask a family member to do the activity with you.

FAITH ALIVE   AT HOME AND IN THE PARISH

In this lesson your fifth grader has learned more about the four marks of the Church. The Church is one, holy, catholic, and apostolic. Beyond a confession of faith, these four marks are challenges that the whole Church and every member is called to live faithfully. Ask your son or daughter to name and describe each mark. Discuss with the family how each of you as a member of the Church can live these marks today. Use this list to help you.

■ We can show that we are *one* with others in our parish by celebrating the Eucharist each week with them. We can pray for the unity of all Christians. We can forgive others.

■ We can show that we are *holy* by loving God, praying frequently, and celebrating the sacraments. We can grow in holiness by treating all people justly and by living in peace with them.

■ We can show that we are *catholic* by welcoming everyone and treating them as important because they, too, are loved by God.

■ We can show that we are *apostolic* by learning how to live our Catholic faith and working for the reign of God. We can pray that the Holy Spirit will guide our pope and bishops. We can ask the Holy Spirit to help us and our parish to carry out the mission of Jesus Christ.

Then do the activity together.

† Family Prayer

May the Holy Spirit help us to show we are holy by loving the people in our family, our parish, and our neighborhood.

Learn by heart Faith Summary

● The marks of the Church are one, holy, catholic, and apostolic.

● The Church of Jesus Christ shows it is one and holy when we are united in faith and live holy lives.

● The Church of Jesus Christ shows it is catholic and apostolic by welcoming all and being faithful to the mission and beliefs Jesus gave to the apostles.

Living Symbol

Choose one of the four marks. Create a symbol that expresses what that sign means to you.

Review

Go over the *Faith Summary* together and encourage your fifth grader to learn it by heart, especially the first statement. Then have him or her do the *Review*. The answers to numbers 1–4 appear on page 216. The response to number 5 will help you see how well your fifth grader is trying to grow in holiness. When the *Review* is completed, go over it together.

Complete the following sentences with the words below.

catholic   **one**   **holy**   **apostolic**

1. We, though many, are made part of the_____
   body of Jesus Christ through Baptism.

2. The second mark of the Church reminds us that we are
   called to be _____.

3. The third mark of the Church reminds us that we are a
   universal, or _____, Church.

4. The fourth mark of the Church, _____, reminds
   us that we are a community founded on the apostles.

5. This week I will help to show that our Church is holy by

   _____

   _____

   _____

FAMILY SCRIPTURE MOMENT

Gather and ask: What beliefs do we share with Christians who are not Catholic? Then **Listen** as Jesus speaks to us of His hope for unity.

The thief comes only in order to steal, kill, and destroy. I have come in order that you might have life—life in all its fullness. I am the good shepherd. As the Father knows Me and I know the Father, in the same way I know My sheep and they know Me. And I am willing to die for them. There are other sheep which belong to Me that are not in this sheep pen. I must bring them, too; they will listen to My voice, and they will become one flock with one shepherd.

From John 10:10, 14–16

Share what each one heard Jesus saying.

Consider for family enrichment:

■ Shepherds often had to save their flock from predators. Jesus, our Good Shepherd, protects us and wants all to belong to His one flock.

■ As members of the one, holy, catholic, and apostolic Church, we welcome all people into our faith community.

Reflect and **Decide** How might we help others outside Jesus' flock to hear His voice? Will we join with people in our parish to reach out to them?

23 ✝ All People Are God's People

Dear Jesus, help us to love one another as You love us.

OUR LIFE

It was almost the last day of the summer Olympics. Some athletes who had just completed the track and field competition were being interviewed for TV.

"Let me ask you," the interviewer said looking at the group that included young people from many different countries. "What is the highlight of this experience for you?"

What do you think was the answer?

The athletes did not talk about competition, or gold medals, or national honor. To a person they said their deepest memory would be of meeting people from different cultures, different backgrounds, different races, different languages, and discovering how very much they all shared in common.

"The Olympic circles are the color of the races of the world," one athlete remarked, "but they are all linked together as one."

What do you think this story says about prejudice?

How do you try to live this "Olympic" dream?

SHARING LIFE

Is there any person or group of people that you find hard to treat as equals? Why is this so? Who can help you?

Discuss together: How does God want you to treat people who are different from you? Explain.

Respecting Other Religions

We meet many people who differ from us in color, religion, age, language, or wealth. Although people are different, all are created in God's image and likeness. We must treat everyone with respect.

Prejudice is a dislike for or hatred of people because they are different from us in race, sex, religion, age, or any other way. The Catholic Church condemns all prejudice as a sin.

God calls us to reject prejudice of any kind. This also includes religious prejudice. This is a dislike for people who worship God differently from the way we do, or who do not worship God at all. There are many religions in the world other than Christianity. Jesus wants us to respect all people, even those who do not believe in Him.

We have a special relationship with the Jewish people. Jesus Himself was a Jew and grew up practicing the Jewish religion. Mary, His mother, Saint Joseph, and the apostles were all devoted Jews. Christians must have a great respect for the Jewish people, who are still God's chosen people.

Christians and Jews share these beliefs:

● Both religions believe in the one true God, who is our creator.

● Both religions read, study, and believe the Jewish Scriptures, which Christians call the Old Testament.

● Both religions follow the Ten Commandments.

Christianity itself is made up of all the baptized disciples of Jesus. Originally, there was only one Church. However, over the centuries, divisions took place among Christians.

Among the Christian Churches that became separated from the Catholic Church are the Eastern Orthodox Churches and the Protestant Churches (for example, the Lutheran and Episcopal). Some other Protestant Churches found in America today include the Baptist, Congregationalist, Methodist, and Presbyterian.

By Baptism all Christians are united as brothers and sisters in Christ. We share many important beliefs:

● We believe in and worship the one true God: Father, Son, and Holy Spirit.

Racism is a sin of prejudice.

● We believe in Jesus Christ, who is both divine and human. Jesus died out of love for us and to save us from our sins. He rose from the dead to bring us new life.

● We believe that the Bible is the inspired word of God.

● We believe in one Baptism for the forgiveness of sins.

● We believe that we are to live the Ten Commandments and the Law of Love, and to carry on Jesus' mission in the world.

● We believe in the resurrection of the dead on the last day and in everlasting life.

Ecumenism is the search for the reunion of the Christian Churches. The Catholic Church is very involved in this work. All of us must work and pray for Christian unity.

Working Against Prejudice

Prejudice of any kind prevents us from living the way Jesus taught. To avoid being guilty of prejudice, we can learn about people whom we consider "different." We can be friendly with the children in our neighborhood or parish or school who are of another color or religion.

As we get older, we can study more about other Christian traditions and about other religions. Learning what they believe and how they worship God can enrich our own faith.

We can talk about our faith to our friends who are not Catholic. We can pray each day that some day all Christians will be united in one Church.

COMING TO FAITH

Discuss: Why does our Catholic faith teach that all prejudice is a sin?

What can we do to avoid prejudice?

Challenge one another to name the beliefs all Christians have in common.

PRACTICING FAITH

Form five groups, each representing a group that faces prejudice. Cut five large circles out of different-colored paper.

Group 1: Our circle stands for the physically and mentally challenged. Things are sometimes harder for us. But we are just like everyone else.

Group 2: Our circle stands for those who face prejudice because of their skin color. Jesus' followers must be "color blind." (Group 2 makes a slit in its circle and joins it with Group 1's.)

Group 3: Our circle stands for those who face prejudice because of their religious beliefs. We know that God loves all people. (Group 3 joins circles with Group 2.)

Group 4: Our circle stands for those who meet prejudice because of gender. Men and women, girls and boys are equal in God's eyes. (Group 4 joins circles with Group 3.)

Group 5: Our circle stands for poor and homeless people. We have very few material things, but Jesus calls us His very own people. (Group 5 joins with Group 4 and Group 1, linking all circles together.)

All: In Christ, there is no east or west,
In Him no north or south,
One great family bound by love
Throughout the whole wide earth!

Talk with your catechist about ways you and your family might use the "Faith Alive" pages. Talk with family members about ways to fight prejudice.

Children are not born prejudiced or bigoted. Others teach them this sin. In this lesson your fifth grader has learned that any kind of prejudice is evil. Our world and our society constantly face the sin of prejudice—racial, religious, gender prejudice, and prejudice against those who are physically or mentally challenged, against the elderly, against the ill, or against the poor. Prejudice is usually the result of ignorance and fear, both of which can be overcome by God's grace and our good will. We must work to ensure that our own lives and our parish are free of all prejudice.

To deepen your fifth grader's respect for and understanding of other religions, invite to your home neighbors who practice other religions. Ask them to talk about and show pictures illustrating what they believe and how they worship God.

† Family Prayer

Talk together about the fact that our natural differences as family members are a blessing for our family. Pray together:

O God, thank You for all the people in my family; for all the gifts that make us different, and for Your grace that makes us one.

Learn by heart Faith Summary

- As Catholics we must fight against prejudice in our lives.
- We respect those who worship God in other religions.
- We have a special bond with the Jewish people. We seek unity with all Christians.

Make a list of friends who worship differently from you. Put a check when you have told a friend why you are proud to be a Catholic, and your friends have told you about their religion.

FRIEND	RELIGION	TALKED ( )

Review

Go over the *Faith Summary* together and encourage your fifth grader to learn it by heart, especially the first statement. Then have him or her do the *Review*. The answers to numbers 1–4 appear on page 216. The response to number 5 will show how well your fifth grader understands the evil of prejudice, and what he or she can do today to help end it. When the *Review* is completed, go over it together.

Circle whether each is True or False. Then make a false statement true.

1. Prejudice is acceptable in some circumstances.   T   F

2. Not all Christians believe in Jesus.   T   F

3. Christians and Jewish people both follow the Ten Commandments.   T   F

4. Ecumenism is the search for unity among all Christians.   T   F

5. Name a group that suffers from prejudice in our society. Tell some ways you will help to end this prejudice.

_____

_____

_____

_____

_____

_____

FAMILY SCRIPTURE MOMENT

Gather and have family members list ways they have "been blind" about other people. Then **Listen** to a gospel story about blindness.

As Jesus was walking along, He saw a man who had been born blind. His disciples asked, "Teacher, whose sin caused him to be born blind? Was it his own or his parents' sin?" Jesus answered, "His blindness has nothing to do with his sins or his parents' sins. He is blind so that God's power might be seen at work in him. As long as it is day, we must do the work of the One who sent Me; night is coming when no one can work. While I am in the world, I am the Light of the World."
From John 9:1–5

Share how Jesus is the Light of the World for each person.

Consider for family enrichment:

■ By assuming that the blind man was disabled through his own or his parents' fault, the disciples showed their own "blindness."

■ Since all people are made in God's image, prejudice toward anyone for any reason is sinful.

Reflect and **Decide** What is our vision of a world without prejudice of any kind? How will we help to make that vision a reality in our parish, our Church, and our nation?

The Gift of Faith

Lord Jesus, we believe that You have the words of eternal life.

Our Life

Jesus said to the people, "I am the bread that came down from heaven. The one who eats this bread will live forever." Many of His followers could not understand this teaching.

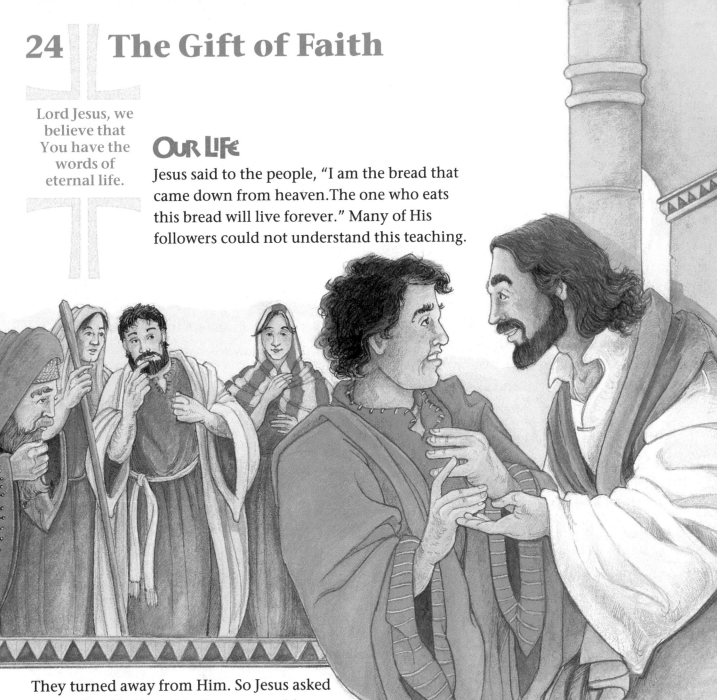

They turned away from Him. So Jesus asked the twelve disciples, "And you—would you also like to leave?"

Simon Peter answered for all of them. "Lord," he said, "to whom would we go? You have the words of eternal life. And now we believe and know that you are the Holy One who has come from God."

From John 6:58, 60, 66–69

What do you learn from this Scripture story?

Suppose Jesus asked you, "Would you also like to leave?" What would be your answer?

Sharing Life

Talk together about these ideas.

- What is it about a person that makes us believe in him or her?
- What is the hardest thing about believing in someone?
- Share the reasons why you believe in God.

OUR CATHOLIC FAITH

The Virtue of Faith

A *virtue* is the habit of doing something good. We find virtues such as courage, honesty, and justice in many people.

In our relationship with God we are asked to practice the special virtues of faith, hope, and love every day. Each of these virtues is a gift from God.

Our Catholic faith is a gift from God. Faith comes to us only because God gives us this gift. We do not earn the gift of faith. In response to God's love, we live our faith as disciples of Jesus Christ and as God's own people.

Jesus is the greatest teacher of our faith. Jesus taught us how to believe and trust in God. Jesus also gave us the Church to help us learn about and live our faith together.

Sometimes it is difficult to understand everything about God and our faith. Many things about God are called mysteries of faith, such as the Blessed Trinity. No one can fully understand these mysteries. We believe them because God has revealed, or made them known, to us. The Church teaches them to us, and they are part of our faith.

Our Church has several prayers called creeds that summarize what we believe. We pray the Nicene Creed at Mass.

On the next page is another creed. It is called the Apostles' Creed because it developed from the very early teachings of the Church. The Apostles' Creed describes the most important truth of our Catholic faith: There is one God but three divine Persons in the one God. We call this truth the mystery of the Blessed Trinity.

Our faith requires that we practice what we believe and put our faith into action. Here are some ways we can do this:

- We should learn as much as we can about our faith.

- We should celebrate the sacraments often, especially Eucharist and Reconciliation.

- We should make decisions each day that show we are living the Law of Love and building up the reign of God.

- We should avoid all forms of prejudice.

- We should try to be peacemakers in our lives and pray for peace in the world.

Perugino, *Consegna delle Chiavi*, Sistine Chapel, Vatican

THE APOSTLE'S CREED

The Apostles' Creed tells the story of God's love for us. It is divided into three parts. The first part of the Apostles' Creed tells us about God the Father, who gives us life.

I believe in God, the Father almighty, creator of heaven and earth.

The second part speaks of God the Son, who became our Savior and the Savior of all people. God the Son became one of us to save us from sin. Jesus died on the cross and rose from the dead to bring us new life. He redeemed us and freed us from the power of sin. He is the perfect sign of God's love for us.

I believe in Jesus Christ,
his only Son, our Lord.
He was conceived by the power
of the Holy Spirit
and born of the Virgin Mary.
He suffered under Pontius Pilate,
was crucified, died, and was buried.
He descended to the dead.
On the third day he rose again.
He ascended into heaven,
and is seated at the right hand of the Father.
He will come again to judge
the living and the dead.

The third part of the Apostles' Creed talks first of God the Holy Spirit, who is our sanctifier, the one who makes us holy.

Then the Creed reminds us that we are to believe that the Church was founded by Jesus. We are in union with all baptized persons, living and dead.

I believe in the Holy Spirit,
the holy, catholic Church,
the communion of saints,
the forgiveness of sins,
the resurrection of the body,
and the life everlasting.
Amen.

We believe that our sins will be forgiven if we are truly sorry for them, and that we will rise again to live with God forever in heaven.

COMING TO FAITH

Take turns sharing what your Catholic faith means to you.

Then help one another remember what the Apostles' Creed teaches us about:

- God the Father.
- God the Son.
- God the Holy Spirit.

PRACTICING FAITH

Do your best to memorize the Apostles' Creed. Try learning two or three lines each day until you have memorized it.

Think about what it means to have faith, to believe in God our loving Creator, in Jesus our Redeemer, and the Holy Spirit our Sanctifier. Then express your faith by drawing a symbol or by writing a poem, or by just writing key words that say what your faith means to you.

Take turns sharing what you have made. Listen carefully as your friends speak. We can help one another strengthen our faith.

✝ Close by praying together the words of the Apostles' Creed.

Talk with your catechist about ways you and your family might use the "Faith Alive" pages. Pray the prayer together.

FAITH ALIVE AT HOME AND IN THE PARISH

In this lesson your fifth grader has learned more about the virtue of faith. This is the first of the three great virtues that are at the core of our Catholic identity. They are sometimes called the theological virtues because they pertain to our relationship with God. Ask her or him to tell you what was learned about the virtue of faith.

Read together the Bible story of Jesus walking on the water (Matthew 14:22–33). In this story Jesus asks Peter to have faith and trust in Him and to walk on the water, too. But Peter doubted Jesus, lost faith, and began to sink. So

Jesus said to him, "What little faith you have! Why did you doubt?" (Matthew 14:31).

As a family, think about the hard times that each family member has faced in trying to practice her or his Christian faith. Then talk about the times that family members, like Peter, relied only on themselves instead of trusting in Jesus' love and care.

Discuss the fact that once we have done the best we can, we have to place ourselves in God's hands, trusting in God's promise of loving care. This is how we and our whole parish practice the virtue of faith.

† Family Prayer

Jesus, we believe in You because You are the way, the truth, and the life. Amen.

Learn by heart Faith Summary

- The virtues of faith, hope, and love are gifts from God.

- Faith is a virtue that enables us to trust and believe in God, to accept what God has revealed, and to live according to God's will.

- The creeds of the Church summarize what we believe.

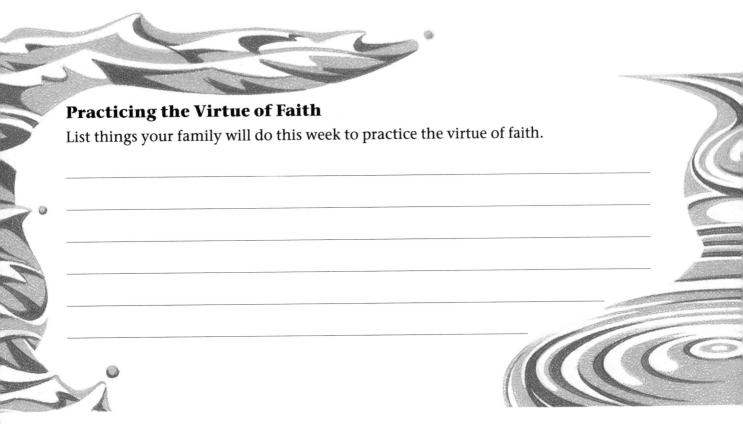

Practicing the Virtue of Faith

List things your family will do this week to practice the virtue of faith.

_____

_____

_____

_____

_____

Review

Go over the *Faith Summary* together and encourage your fifth grader to learn it by heart, especially the first two statements. Then have him or her do the *Review*. The answers to numbers 1–4 appear on page 216. The response to number 5 will show how well your fifth grader accepts responsibility for living the faith. When the *Review* is completed, go over it together.

Circle the letter beside the correct answer.

1. The habit of doing good is called
   a. a sacrament.
   b. a virtue.
   c. the Apostles' Creed.
   d. a mystery.

2. A mystery is something we do not fully
   a. pray about.
   b. learn about.
   c. understand.
   d. care about.

3. Faith enables us to
   a. trust and believe in God.
   b. accept what God has revealed.
   c. live according to God's loving will.
   d. all of the above

4. The Apostles' Creed includes
   a. Jesus walking on water.
   b. the virtue of love.
   c. the mystery of the Blessed Trinity.
   d. the virtue of hope.

5. How will you show this week that you accept the responsibility to live your Christian faith?

_____

_____

_____

FAMILY SCRIPTURE MOMENT

Gather and have family members name persons and things in which they have faith and tell why. Then **Listen** to the story of doubting Thomas.

The other disciples told Thomas, "We have seen the Lord!" Thomas said, "Unless I see the scars of the nails in His hands and put my finger on those scars and my hand in His side, I will not believe." A week later, Jesus came and said, "Peace be with you." Then He said to Thomas, "Put your finger here, and look at My hands; then reach out your hand and put it in My side. Stop your doubting, and believe!" Thomas answered, "My Lord and my God!" Jesus said to him, "Do you believe because you see Me? How happy are those who believe without seeing Me!"
From John 20:25–29

Share what family members heard in this reading for their own lives.

Consider for family enrichment:

■ Thomas is afraid to believe in the good news of Jesus' resurrection.

■ Jesus praises all who, like us, believe in Him without demanding that we first see His glorified body.

Reflect and **Decide** What can we as a family do to deepen our faith in Jesus? Pray together: "My Lord and my God!"

25 ✝ God Fills Us with Hope

Jesus, we place all our hope in You.

Our Life

Pope John Paul II loves young people. He enjoys being with them and hearing what they have to say about their lives and about their faith. He always brings them a message of hope.

After meeting with the Holy Father, here is what a group of young people had to say:

"I think the pope is great! He makes me feel that things are better than I thought."

"Wow! He told us how much the Church needs us and how important we are. That's cool!"

"He told us that we are the future of the Church. He made me feel that young people like us can make a difference."

Do you know anyone who is filled with hope? Tell about him or her.

What do you think it means to be a person of hope?

What does hope mean in your life now?

Sharing Life

Have you ever been in a situation in which you felt hopeless? Tell about it. Explain what you did and why.

Talk together and share reasons why Christians should always have hope.

The Virtue of Hope

Often we use the word hope to mean "wish and expect." When we say, "I hope it will be nice this weekend," we are wishing for good weather. The virtue of hope means much more than this kind of wishing or expecting.

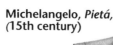

Michelangelo, *Pietá,* (15th century)

We practice the virtue of hope when we trust that God will help us in every situation, no matter what our problem is.

Hope, like faith, is a gift from God. We are able to have hope because God promises to love us always. Our confidence in God helps us to live as people with hope.

Jesus is our greatest source of hope. We trust in Jesus' promise that our actions will make a difference. When Christians hope that God's reign will really come, we are not just wishing. We do all that we can each day to make it happen. With the help of the Holy Spirit, we do our best to do God's loving will, knowing that our lives can make a difference.

Everyday we read about sadness and suffering. We are tempted to wonder whether God has forgotten us. To hope does not mean to wait for God to solve all our problems. With the help of God's grace, we must work together for the reign of God.

Two thousand years ago, Saint Paul also lived in a world filled with problems. Christians were being persecuted and killed for their faith in Jesus Christ. It looked as if the Church, which had just begun, would not last.

Saint Paul wrote to the Christians in Rome to encourage them to have hope:

"There is nothing in all creation that will ever be able to separate us from the love of God which is ours through Christ Jesus our Lord"(Romans 8:39).

Hope is a virtue that enables us to trust that God will be with us in every situation.

Mary, A Sign of Hope

Mary is a special sign of hope for us. The Blessed Virgin Mary was Jesus' first and greatest disciple. Mary is the Mother of the Church.

The Church teaches that at the end of her life, Jesus brought Mary, body and soul, to be with Him forever in heaven. We call this Mary's assumption. We celebrate this event on August 15. Mary's assumption strengthens our hope that we, too, will live forever in heaven.

We can ask Mary to help us hope that we can make things better in the world. Then one day our hope will be fulfilled. We, too, like Mary, will enjoy life with God forever in heaven.

The Church today continues to bring a message of hope to the whole world. Each time we pray and celebrate the sacraments with our parish community, we show that we have hope that God's reign will come.

167

COMING TO FAITH

As Christians we can show hope in God in many ways. Discuss what you would do to live the virtue of hope in each of these situations. Why?

- Everything at home seems hopeless. No one seems to understand you. You feel like running away.
- People are being treated unfairly and with prejudice because of their race or religion.
- Violence seems to be a way of life; young people are losing their lives on our streets.

PRACTICING FAITH

Share with one another ways you can be signs of hope in your homes and neighborhood. Write on the candle one way you will do this. Then gather in a circle with your friends. Take turns holding up your candle and reading aloud your decision of hope. Pray together:

†**Leader:** Let us pray for hope for others and for ourselves.

All: We are people of hope.

Leader: God, our Creator, help those who have given up hope.

All: We are people of hope.

Leader: Jesus Christ, our Redeemer, help those who suffer from addiction. Free them from their hopeless actions.

All: We are people of hope.

Leader: Holy Spirit, our Sanctifier, help all people, especially those our age, who want to hurt themselves or even end their lives. Take away their hopelessness.

All: We are people of hope.

Leader: Loving God, help each one of us to be a person of hope.

All: Amen.

Talk with your catechist about ways you and your family might use the "Faith Alive" pages.

FAITH ALIVE
AT HOME AND IN THE PARISH

In this lesson your fifth grader has learned more about the virtue of hope. Ask him or her to tell you what hope means and how to live it each day at home and in the parish.

As Christians, we usually know when we sin against faith or love, but we are not nearly as conscious of sins against hope. Yet hope, too, is one of the great and central virtues of our faith.

Help your family to understand that in Christian faith, the life, death, and resurrection of Jesus are our greatest source of hope. Because of Easter, we know that Jesus will help us to avoid sin and do God's loving will. We can live in hope because we know that we can always rely on God.

Discuss as a family how you feel about news items you see, hear, or read that report situations which appear to be hopeless.

Share how your family feels about the life, death, and resurrection of Jesus as the greatest source of hope for our world. To help your fifth grader see this, read or tell the Bible story of when Jesus appeared to Mary Magdalene and told her to tell everyone He had been raised from the dead (John 20:1–18).

Then talk about things your family can say and do to be a sign of hope. Help your family look to Mary as a sign of hope by doing the activity below together.

† Family Prayer

O Mary, help us never to give up on your Son's love. We have hope that His kingdom will come, and that we will live forever with Him in heaven.

Honoring Mary

Design a banner honoring Our Lady, an example of hope for all Christians.

Learn by heart Faith Summary

- Hope is the virtue that enables us to trust that God will be with us in every situation.

- Jesus is our greatest source of hope.

- Mary, the Mother of the Church, is a sign of hope for us.

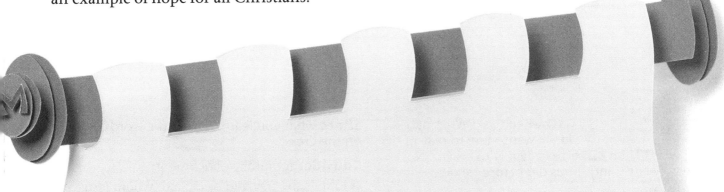

Review

Go over the *Faith Summary* together and encourage your fifth grader to learn it by heart, especially the first two statements. Then have him or her do the *Review*. The answers to numbers 1–4 appear on page 216. The response to number 5 will help you see how well your fifth grader is growing as a person of hope. When the *Review* is completed, go over it together.

Circle the letter beside the correct answer.

1. Hope enables us to

    a. trust in God's promises.

    b. doubt God's promises.

    c. worry about God's promises.

    d. deny God's promises.

2. On August 15, Catholics celebrate

    a. Pentecost.

    b. Christmas.

    c. the birth of Mary.

    d. the Assumption.

3. Jesus' first and greatest disciple is

    a. Saint Peter.

    b. Mary.

    c. Saint Paul.

    d. Saint John the Baptist.

4. We can be signs of hope by

    a. praying.

    b. celebrating the sacraments.

    c. trying our best to do God's loving will.

    d. all of the above

5. What will you do to show you are a person of hope?

_____

_____

_____

_____

_____

FAMILY SCRIPTURE MOMENT

Gather and ask: What part do we want Mary to play in our lives? Then **Listen** as a family to one of the very last things Jesus did before He died on the cross.

Standing close to Jesus' cross were His mother, His mother's sister, and Mary Magdalene. Jesus saw His mother and the disciple He loved standing there; so He said to His mother, "He is your son." Then He said to the disciple, "She is your mother." From that time the disciple took her to live in his home. Jesus knew that by now everything had been completed. Then He said, "It is finished." He bowed His head and gave up His spirit.

From John 19:25–28, 30

Share what you learned from the words of Jesus on the cross.

Consider for family enrichment:

■ John is the beloved disciple to whom Jesus entrusts His mother. John is the symbol of the entire Church; Mary is to be the mother of us all.

■ Mary is a sign of hope to us that we, too, will conquer death and live forever with the risen Lord.

Reflect and **Decide** What might we do to make Mary an ever-present member of our family? Pray together: Thank You, Lord, for sharing Your mother with us.

Jesus, help us to love others as You love us.

Our Life

The apostle John once wrote a long letter to the Christians of the early Church. He was concerned that some might be overcome by the pressures of the world and forget the most important teaching of Jesus' way of life.

What do you think is the most important teaching of Jesus about the way we should live?

Here is a part of John's letter. Listen to it as if he is writing it directly to you.

Dear friends,
Let us love one another because love comes from God. Whoever loves is a child of God and knows God. Whoever does not love does not know God, for God is love.... This is what love is: it is not that we have loved God, but that God has loved us, and sent the Son to forgive our sins.

Dear friends, if this is how God loved us, then we should love one another.

From 1 John 4:7–11

What did you hear from John's letter for your life?

John uses the word *love* ten times! What do you think John means by *love*?

Sharing Life

Discuss: how can we love those who are
- strangers to us?
- different from us?

What does Jesus, and John, expect of us when they say "love one another"?

WALK FOR HUNGER

The Virtue of Love

The virtue of love is one of God's greatest gifts to us. Because we are created in God's image and likeness, we are made to love and be loved. Living the virtue of love is what makes us most like God.

We practice the virtue of love not just with words and feelings, but especially by what we do for others. We should not give to others or do for others only when it is convenient for us. To live the virtue of love we must often sacrifice, or give up something, to show our love for God and others.

Jesus' whole life was an act of love. He once told His followers this powerful story to help them better understand how important the virtue of love is in living for God's reign.

Jesus said that at the end of time He will say, "Come all of you that are blessed. Come into the kingdom that has been prepared for you ever since the creation of the world."

"When I was hungry, you fed Me, thirsty and you gave Me a drink. I was a stranger and you took Me into your homes. I was naked and you gave Me clothes. I was sick and you took care of Me, in prison and you visited Me."

The followers will ask, "When did we do all these things for you?"

Jesus will reply, "I tell you, whenever you did this for one of the least important of My brothers and sisters, you did it for Me!"

From Matthew 25:31–46

Jesus was teaching His disciples that love demands action. The virtue of love demands that we reach out to others, especially to people in need. The true love that Jesus taught us demands that we treat others fairly and with justice.

Love is a virtue that enables us to love God, our neighbor, and ourselves.

The Greatest Virtue

In our Catholic tradition, we know some very specific ways to practice the virtue of love. These are called the Corporal and Spiritual Works of Mercy.

The Corporal Works of Mercy show us how to care for the physical well-being of our neighbors. The Spiritual Works of Mercy show us how to care for their spiritual well-being.

When we practice the virtue of love, we come to know why Saint Paul ends his description of love by saying that of the three virtues of faith, hope, and love, "the greatest of these is love" (1 Corinthians 13:13).

Corporal Works of Mercy
- Feed the hungry.
- Give drink to the thirsty.
- Shelter the homeless.
- Clothe the naked.
- Care for the sick.
- Help the imprisoned.
- Bury the dead.

Spiritual Works of Mercy
- Share knowledge.
- Give advice to those who need it.
- Comfort those who suffer.
- Be patient with others.
- Forgive those who hurt you.
- Give correction to those who need it.
- Pray for others.

COMING TO FAITH

Rewrite these Corporal and Spiritual Works of Mercy as action statements so that it is easier for you to practice them. For example, you could rewrite "Comfort those who suffer" as "I can invite someone who is suffering from prejudice to spend time with my group of friends."

MY ACTION PLAN

Share knowledge.

_____

_____

_____

Be patient with others.

_____

_____

_____

Feed the hungry.

_____

_____

_____

Shelter the homeless.

_____

_____

_____

Pray for others.

_____

_____

_____

PRACTICING FAITH

Talk together about a work of mercy that you might take on as a group project this coming week. For example:

● Does your parish work for the poor and homeless? How can you help?

● Could a catechist use some help with younger children?

Plan what you can do. Then do it! End by listening again to the words from Saint John's letter on page 171.

Talk with your catechist about ways you and your family might use the "Faith Alive" pages. Pray the family prayer with your catechist and friends.

FAITH ALIVE

AT HOME AND IN THE PARISH

In this lesson your fifth grader has learned more about the greatest virtue of all, love. Ask her or him to tell you what Jesus and John mean by love. Know that in our Catholic tradition love always demands justice; true love means much more than a sentimental feeling.

As a family read and talk about this description of real love written by Saint Paul:

Love is patient and kind; it is not jealous or conceited or proud; love is not ill-mannered or selfish or irritable; love does not keep a record of wrongs; love is not happy with evil, but is happy with the truth. Love never gives up; and its faith, hope, and patience never fail.

From 1 Corinthians 13:4–7

Discuss with your fifth grader ways you and your parish can live the virtue of love. Conclude by helping to complete this activity.

† Family Prayer

O God, we love You above all things. Help us to love one another and ourselves as Jesus taught us to do.

Growing in Love

During vacation keep a weekly calendar. Write one way you will try to practice the virtue of love each day. Use the Spiritual and Corporal Works of Mercy for suggestions.

Learn by heart Faith Summary

● Love is a virtue that enables us to love God, our neighbor, and ourselves.

● The Corporal and Spiritual Works of Mercy are some very specific ways to practice the virtue of love.

● Saint Paul tells us that love is the greatest Christian virtue.

Monday
_____
_____

Sunday
_____
_____

Tuesday
_____
_____

Wednesday
_____
_____

Thursday
_____
_____

Friday
_____

Saturday
_____
_____

Review

Circle the letter beside the correct answer.

1. Saint Paul said the greatest virtue is
   a. hope.
   b. love.
   c. faith.
   d. truth.

2. By His example, Jesus revealed that we practice love in our
   a. words.
   b. feelings.
   c. actions.
   d. all of the above

3. The Corporal Works of Mercy include
   a. praying for others.
   b. comforting those who suffer.
   c. caring for the sick.
   d. sharing knowledge.

4. The Spiritual Works of Mercy include
   a. forgiving those who hurt you.
   b. feeding the hungry.
   c. caring for the sick.
   d. sheltering the homeless.

5. How will you practice the virtue of love this week?

   _____

   _____

   _____

   _____

   _____

FAMILY SCRIPTURE MOMENT

Gather and have each person tell a story about a time someone showed him or her genuine love. Ask: How do people who truly love us affect who we are? Then **Listen** as Jesus gives us a new commandment.

Jesus said, "My children, I shall not be with you very much longer. You will look for Me; but I tell you now what I told the Jewish authorities, 'You cannot go where I am going.' And now I give you a new commandment: love one another. As I have loved you, so you must love one another. If you have love for one another, then everyone will know that you are My disciples."
John 13:33–35

Share the signs by which people know that you are Jesus' disciples.

Consider for family enrichment:

■ In the Old Testament, God had commanded, "You shall love your neighbor as yourself" (Leviticus 19:18). At the Last Supper Jesus adds that His disciples must love as He has loved them.

■ We show that we are Christians by our love.

Reflect and **Decide** As a family, what attitudes or habits prevent us from loving as Jesus loved? What first step will we take in overcoming these obstacles?

27 | Sacramentals

Jesus help us to see signs of Your love in our daily lives.

OUR LIFE

Our country honors people in many ways. One special way is by placing statues of two people from each state in the National Statuary Hall located in the Capitol building in Washington, D.C. Among those selected for this honor are thirteen Catholics—so far.

Father Damian of Molokai

Arizona: Father Eusebio Kino, Jesuit

California: Father Junipero Serra, Franciscan

Hawaii: Father Damian of Molokai, Sacred Heart Fathers

Illinois: General James Shields

Louisiana: Justice Edward D. White

Maryland: Charles Carroll

Nevada: Patrick A. McCarren

New Mexico: Dennis Chavez

North Dakota: John Burke

Oregon: Dr. John McLoughlin

Washington: Mother Mary Joseph Pariseau, Sister of Charity of Providence

West Virginia: John E. Kenna

Wisconsin: Father Jacques Marquette, Jesuit

Do you know why any one of these Catholics is honored this way?

What things do you or your family have that remind you of someone?

SHARING LIFE

What things in your parish church help you to remember Jesus, or Mary, and the saints?

Why are these things a help?

Sacramentals

There are many things in our daily lives that remind us of God. Our Church uses blessings, actions, and objects to help us remember God, Jesus, Mary, and the saints. We call these *sacramentals*.

We bless ourselves with *holy water* as we enter the church. Holy water is a sacramental that reminds us that we have been baptized by water and the Holy Spirit and have become God's own children.

The *altar* in our church is also a sacramental. The altar is the symbol of Jesus Christ. It is sometimes called the Lord's table because it reminds us of the Last Supper.

We may wear a *cross* to help us remember the death and resurrection of Jesus. Or we may wear a *medal* to help us remember Mary or the saints. Looking at a *statue* of Jesus, Mary, or one of the saints while we are praying helps us to remember their love and care for us.

We also use sacramentals during the liturgical year. We light *Advent candles* to help us remember that Christ is the Light of the World. On Ash Wednesday we receive *ashes* on our foreheads. This reminds us to turn away from sin and to turn to the good news of Jesus. On Good Friday we kiss the *crucifix* as a sign of respect and love for Jesus crucified.

During the Easter season we light the *Paschal*, or *Easter Candle* to remember the resurrection of Jesus.

The Rosary

The *rosary* is also a sacramental. Praying the rosary helps us to remember the lives of Jesus and Mary.

We begin praying the rosary with the sign of the cross. The rosary has a cross on which we then pray the Apostles' Creed and remember the beliefs of our faith. The cross is followed by one large bead and three smaller beads. We pray the Our Father on the large bead and one Hail Mary on each of the small beads.

Then there is a circle of five groups of beads, or "decades." Each decade has one large bead and ten smaller ones. We pray an Our Father on each of the large beads and one Hail Mary on each of the small beads. We end each decade by praying the Glory to the Father.

As we pray the rosary, we think about the joyful, sorrowful, and glorious events in the lives of Jesus and Mary. We call these the mysteries of the rosary. There are fifteen mysteries of the rosary. They are:

The Five Joyful Mysteries

1. The annunciation
2. The visitation
3. The birth of Jesus
4. The presentation of Jesus in the Temple
5. The finding of Jesus in the Temple

The Five Sorrowful Mysteries

1. The agony in the garden
2. The scourging at the pillar
3. The crowning with thorns
4. The carrying of the cross
5. The crucifixion and death

The Five Glorious Mysteries

1. The resurrection
2. The ascension
3. The descent of the Holy Spirit upon the apostles
4. The assumption of Mary into heaven
5. The coronation of Mary as Queen of heaven

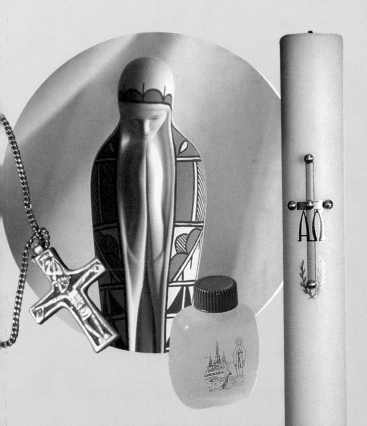

Saint Frances Cabrini

COMING TO FAITH

How do sacramentals help you to remember God's presence in your life?

Name a sacramental that you have learned about. Tell what it helps you to remember.

_____

_____

Draw a picture or a symbol of your favorite sacramental. Then gather together and share your ideas.

PRACTICING FAITH

Statues and medals remind us of the saints who were faithful disciples of Jesus. Their lives can encourage us and remind us of how we can live our faith today.

Read about the saints below and then share together your ideas about ways you can be like them, faithful followers of Jesus Christ.

Saint Thomas More (1478–1535) was a devoted husband, parent, and a successful lawyer. He rose to great power in the government of England when Henry VIII was king. But Henry VIII made himself the head of the Church in England and demanded that Thomas More take an oath against the pope. Thomas refused and was sentenced to death. Thomas More remained loyal both to the Church and to England. He said, "I am the king's good servant, but God's first."

What quality in Thomas More's life will help you to live as Jesus' disciple?

_____

_____

Saint Frances Cabrini (1850–1917) was an orphan who became a school teacher. Frances Cabrini founded the Missionary Sisters of the Sacred Heart to teach orphaned children in Italy. She and some of her Missionary Sisters came to America in 1889. In America Frances founded many schools, orphanages, and hospitals to help the immigrants.

What quality in Frances Cabrini's life will help you to live as Jesus' disciple?

_____

_____

Another saint I like is _____

The quality I admire and will try to imitate in this saint's life is

_____

_____

Talk with your catechist about ways you and your family can use the "Faith Alive" pages together. Pray the Our Father with your catechist and friends.

FAITH ALIVE AT HOME AND IN THE PARISH

In this lesson your fifth grader learned that sacramentals are blessings, actions, or objects that help us remember God, Jesus, Mary, the saints, and our call to discipleship. Sacramentals include, for example, blessings, medals, relics, shrines, blessed water, candles, palms and ashes, rosary beads and stations of the cross. They are material, visible realities that help us to be more aware of the invisible loving presence of God, Mary, and the saints in our lives.

We do not worship or pray to sacramentals. Rather, we look to the reality for which they stand. They help us see that all of life can be holy. Sacramentals enrich our Christian life by directing attention to God, who speaks to us through all the gifts of God's creation. Talk to your family about sacramentals and encourage family members to use and treat sacramentals with reverence and respect.

†Family Prayer

Thank You, dear God, for filling our lives with Your presence. With Your grace, let all things remind us of You.

Learn by heart Faith Summary

● Sacramentals are blessings, actions, and objects that remind us of God, Jesus, Mary, and the saints.

● The rosary is a sacramental that helps us reflect on the lives of Jesus and Mary.

Sacramentals

Do you have any sacramentals in your home? Do a search and make a list of what you find. If you have none, talk together as a family about having and using sacramentals as a part of your Christian family life.

Review

Go over the *Faith Summary* together and encourage your fifth grader to learn it by heart, especially the first statement. Then have him or her complete the *Review*. The answers to numbers 1–4 appear on page 216. The response to number 5 will indicate your child's understanding of sacramentals and how they help us live our faith. When the *Review* is completed, go over it together.

Complete these sentences about sacramentals.

1. _____ reminds us that we have become God's children in Baptism.

2. The _____ reminds us of Jesus' suffering and death on the cross.

3. We light the _____ to remember the resurrection of Jesus.

4. We receive _____ on our foreheads at the beginning of Lent to remind us to turn from sin.

5. How can sacramentals help us live our faith?

_____

_____

_____

_____

_____

_____

FAMILY SCRIPTURE MOMENT

Gather around a lighted candle and ask: How is Jesus the light of my world? Then **Listen** as a family to one of Jesus' descriptions of Himself.

Jesus spoke to the Pharisees and said, "I am the light of the world. Whoever follows Me will have the light of life and will never walk in darkness." The Pharisees said, "Now You are testifying on Your own behalf." Jesus answered, "It is written in your law that when two witnesses agree, what they say is true. I testify on My own behalf, and the Father who sent Me also testifies on My behalf."

From John 8:12–13, 17–18

Share Have family members name things in the home, the church, or the community that remind them of Jesus.

Consider for family enrichment:
■ In John's Gospel, Jesus is repeatedly identified with the image of light.
■ Candles are a beautiful sacramental of Jesus' light among us.

Reflect Does our home reflect our faith by the presence of sacramentals?

Decide Light a candle and give one another a blessing: "May the light of Christ shine in your life!"

182

God, we remember and celebrate all the gifts of Your love.

Mass of the Holy Spirit

Opening Hymn:
Write title here.

_____

First Reading
The Holy Spirit comes to the disciples as Jesus promised. (Read Acts 2:1–11.)

Responsorial Psalm
Choose an appropriate psalm from the Lectionary or Bible, for example—Psalm 23 or Psalm 145. Write your selection here.

_____

Response: Lord, send out Your Spirit, and renew the face of the earth.

Gospel
A reading from the holy gospel according to John. (Read John 20:19–23.)

Prayer of the Faithful
Leader: Come, Holy Spirit. Renew the face of the earth.

All: Come, Holy Spirit. Renew the face of the earth. *(This response is said after each of the following)*

Reader: Come, Holy Spirit. Give us the gift of wisdom.

All: (Response)

Reader: Come, Holy Spirit. Give us the gift of understanding.

All: (Response)

Reader: Come, Holy Spirit. Give us the gift of right judgment.

All: (Response)

Reader: Come, Holy Spirit. Give us the gift of courage.

All: (Response)

Reader: Come, Holy Spirit. Give us the gift of true knowledge.

All: (Response)

Reader: Come, Holy Spirit. Give us the gift of reverence.

All: (Response)

Reader: Come, Holy Spirit. Give us the gift of wonder and awe in Your presence.

All: (Response)

Reader: Come, Holy Spirit. Fill our hearts with Your gifts, and come upon us as You came upon the disciples on the first Pentecost.

All: Amen.

Presentation of the Gifts
Write the names of those who will carry the bread and wine to the altar.

Gift	Presenter
_____	_____
_____	_____
_____	_____

Communion Hymn

Closing Hymn

A Way of the Cross

Act One: Arrest and Sentencing

All: *Sing an appropriate song.*

Leader: A reading from the holy gospel according to Mark.(Read Mark 14:43–46.)

First Station

Reader: The next day Pontius Pilate sentenced You, Jesus, to be crucified. You always did God's will and lived to bring about the reign of God. Help us when others make fun of us and ignore us for doing God's loving will.

All: We adore You, O Christ, and we praise You, because by Your holy cross You have redeemed the world.

Second Station

Reader: Jesus, the soldiers made fun of You. They placed a crown of thorns on Your head and laughed at You. Help us when others make fun of us because we are living the Law of Love.

All: *Repeat response "We adore You…."*

Third Station

Reader: Jesus, You are the Son of God and one of us. The cross became too heavy and You fell under it. Help us when others tempt us to disobey the Ten Commandments. (Response)

Think and Decide:

What will you do to show that you are proud to be a disciple of Jesus?

Act Two: Helpers Along the Way

All: *Sing an appropriate song.*

Leader: A reading from the holy gospel according to Luke.(Read Luke 23:26–27.)

Fourth Station

Reader: Jesus, Your mother, Mary, sees and shares in Your pain and suffering. Help us turn to Mary, our mother, for strength to live as Your disciples. (Response)

Fifth Station

Reader: Jesus, the soldiers order Simon to help You carry Your cross. Help us to bring freedom to those suffering from injustice. (Response)

Sixth Station

Reader: Jesus, Veronica wipes the blood and sweat from Your face. Help us to live the Works of Mercy. (Response)

Seventh Station

Reader: Jesus, the weight of the cross causes You to fall a second time. May the Holy Spirit help us to live Your Law of Love. (Response)

Eighth Station

Reader: Jesus, You tell a group of women from Jerusalem to have hope in Your promises. Help us to trust in all God's promises. (Response)

Think and Decide:

What will you do to show that you are proud to be a disciple of Jesus?

Act Three: Darkness Over the Earth

All: *Sing an appropriate song.*

Leader: A reading from the holy gospel according to Luke.(Read Luke 23:32–34.)

Ninth Station

Reader: Jesus, You fall a third and final time on Your way to Calvary. Give us strength in the Eucharist. (Response)

Tenth Station

Reader: Jesus, the soldiers stripped You and divided Your clothes among themselves. Help us to forgive those who hurt us. (Response)

Eleventh Station

Reader: Jesus, the soldiers crucified You like a criminal. You asked the Father to forgive them. Help us to appreciate Your love for us. (Response)

Twelfth Station

Leader: A reading from the holy gospel according to Luke.(Read Luke 23:44–46.)

Reader: Kneel and ask yourself: "How do I feel about Jesus dying out of love for me?"

Think and Decide:

What will you do to show that you are proud to be a disciple of Jesus?

Act Four: From Death to Life
Thirteenth Station

Reader: Jesus, Your disciples must have felt their dreams were shattered when Joseph of Arimathea took Your lifeless body down from the cross. Help us to see the signs of God's life around us. (Response)

Fourteenth Station

Reader: Jesus, as they buried Your body, the disciples must have felt that their hopes were being buried, too. Help us to see the signs of God's love around us. (Response)

Leader: A reading from the holy gospel according to John. (Read John 20:11–18.)

Think and Decide:

What will you do to be a sign of God's life and love?

All: *Sing an appropriate Easter song.*

Entrance Procession

You may carry flowers that you have bought, made, or grown. Put them on or next to the place that has been set up to honor Mary, our Immaculate Mother.

Opening Hymn

"Immaculate Mary"

Leader: Today, we honor the Blessed Virgin Mary as the woman God chose to be the Mother of God's own Son. We remember that the Immaculate Conception means that Mary was always sinless, even before she was born. We honor Mary as the patroness of our country on December 8, the feast of the Immaculate Conception.

In our litany prayer today, we pray to Mary, using some of the titles with which the Church honors her. These titles help us to remember Mary's role in God's plan of salvation.

Leader: Holy Mary,

All: O Mary, conceived without sin, pray for us who have recourse to you. *(This response is said after each of the following.)*

Leader: Holy Mother of God,
Mother of Christ,
Mother most pure,
Mother most lovable,
Mother of our Creator,
Mother of our Savior,
Virgin most faithful,
Cause of our joy,
Health of the sick,
Refuge of sinners,
Comfort of the afflicted,
Help of Christians,
Queen of angels,
Queen of apostles,
Queen of martyrs,
Queen of all saints,
Queen conceived without
original sin,
Queen of the most holy rosary,
Queen of peace.
Pray for us, Holy Mother of God.

All: That we may be made worthy of the promises of Christ.

Time for Reflection

Choose one of the titles of Mary used in the litany prayer. Think about how it can help you to live as Jesus' disciple today.

Title _____

I will live as a disciple of Jesus by

_____

_____

_____

Closing Hymn

"Sing of Mary"

SUMMARY 2 ▪ REVIEW

Chapter 15—Jesus Christ Forgives Us (Reconciliation)

- Reconciliation is the sacrament in which Jesus Christ shares with us God's mercy and forgiveness of our sins.

- Examination of conscience, contrition, confession, penance, and absolution are important steps in the celebration of Reconciliation.

- In Reconciliation we receive God's help to do God's loving will, to avoid sin, and to live as God's people.

Chapter 16—Jesus Christ Helps Us in Sickness and Death (Anointing of the Sick)

- The sacrament of Anointing of the Sick brings God's special blessings to those who are sick, elderly, or dying.

- Anointing of the Sick is one of the two sacraments of healing.

- We must respect our bodies by caring for them. We must work to eliminate sickness and evil from the world.

Chapter 17—Jesus Christ Helps Us to Love (Matrimony)

- The sacrament of Matrimony is a powerful and effective sign of Christ's presence that joins a man and woman together for life.

- Married couples promise to serve each other and the whole Church. Matrimony is a sacrament of service.

- We can prepare now for Matrimony by trying to love others as God loves us.

Chapter 18—Jesus Christ Calls Us to Serve (Holy Orders)

- Jesus chose twelve apostles to lead our Church in teaching and worship.

- Bishops, priests, and deacons are ordained in the sacrament of Holy Orders.

- Our ordained ministers lead us in building up the Christian community.

Chapter 19—We Share Jesus Christ's Priesthood (Ministry)

- Jesus calls each of us to a specific vocation to carry on His priestly mission.

- Evangelization means spreading the good news of Jesus Christ and sharing our faith by our words and deeds.

- There are many vocations—married, ordained, religious, and single life. We are called to carry on Jesus' mission.

SUMMARY 2 ▪ REVIEW

Chapter 22—Becoming a Catholic (Marks of the Church)

- The marks of the Church are one, holy, catholic, and apostolic.

- The Church of Jesus Christ shows it is one and holy when we are united in faith and live holy lives.

- The Church of Jesus Christ shows it is catholic and apostolic by welcoming all and being faithful to the mission and beliefs Jesus gave to the apostles.

Chapter 23—All People Are God's People

- As Catholics we must fight against prejudice in our lives.

- We respect those who worship God in other religions.

- We have a special bond with the Jewish people. We seek unity with all Christians.

Chapter 24—We Believe in God

- The virtues of faith, hope, and love are gifts from God.

- Faith is a virtue that enables us to trust and believe in God, to accept what God has revealed, and to live according to God's will.

- The creeds of our Church summarize what we believe.

Chapter 25—God Fills Us With Hope

- Hope is the virtue that enables us to trust that God will be with us in every situation.

- Jesus is our greatest source of hope.

- Mary, the Mother of the Church, is a sign of hope for us.

Chapter 26—The Gift of God's Love

- Love is a virtue that enables us to love God, our neighbor, and ourselves.

- The Corporal and Spiritual Works of Mercy are some very specific ways to practice the virtue of love.

- Saint Paul tells us that love is the greatest virtue.

SUMMARY 2 ▪ TEST

Circle the correct answer.

1. The love of married couples is
   a. not celebrated in a special sacrament.
   b. a sign of God's love in the world.
   c. not meant to last forever.
   d. meant only for them.

2. The ordained men who share in Jesus' priestly ministry are
   a. only priests.
   b. only priests and bishops.
   c. priests, bishops, and deacons.
   d. only bishops.

3. The Church is one means
   a. we receive the good news from the apostles.
   b. we welcome all people to our Church.
   c. all baptized persons are united together with Jesus Christ.
   d. we share in God's own life.

4. The virtues of faith, hope, and love are
   a. gifts from God that help us to believe, trust, and love.
   b. sacraments of the Church.
   c. parts of the Mass.
   d. prayers to say.

5. Our most important source of hope is
   a. our vocation.
   b. our bishops, priests, and deacons.
   c. our knowledge.
   d. the resurrection of Jesus Christ.

Complete the following sentences with the words below.

lifelong	Jewish	Sin
bishops	pope	Trinity
priests	contrition	hope

6. Examination of conscience, confession, _____ , penance, and absolution are important parts of Reconciliation.

7. _____ is freely choosing to do what we know is wrong. We disobey God's law on purpose.

8. A man and woman enter into a _____ covenant of love when they celebrate the sacrament of Matrimony.

9. The apostles appointed successors whom we call _____.

10. Bishops ordain _____ to help them.

11. The _____ is the leader of the whole Church. He is the successor of Saint Peter and is the Bishop of Rome.

12. We have a special relationship with the _____ people and we share many beliefs with them.

13. The Apostles' Creed teaches us about the Blessed _____.

14. Mary, the Mother of our Church, is a sign of _____ for us.

SUMMARY 2 ▪ TEST

15. Number the following in the order in which they occur in the Individual Rite of Reconciliation.

_____ The priest gives you absolution.

_____ The priest welcomes you.

_____ You pray an Act of Contrition.

_____ You confess your sins.

_____ The priest tells you to go in peace.

_____ You make the sign of the cross.

_____ You or the priest reads from the Bible.

_____ The priest talks to you about ways to be a better Christian, and he gives you a penance.

Answer the following.

16. In what ways can you celebrate the sacrament of Reconciliation?

_____

_____

_____

17. How can you continue Jesus' mission of healing?

_____

_____

_____

18. How can you prepare now for your vocation in life?

_____

_____

_____

19. How do you see the sacrament of Holy Orders at work?

_____

_____

_____

_____

20. How can you show that you share in the priesthood of Jesus?

_____

_____

_____

Think and decide:

Tell how you will live one of the marks of the Church.

Mark of the Church

_____

I will

_____

DAY OF RETREAT

Theme: Living the Law of Love

◀ OPENING ACTIVITY ▶

During your retreat this year, you will think about who you are and how you want to live your life as a disciple of Jesus. Imagine you could be anyone or anything for one day.

For example:

- an animal
- a star athlete
- a famous entertainer
- other _____

_____

- a musical instrument
- a world leader
- a leader of our Church
- an automobile

Who or what would you choose to be? Write it here and explain why._____

_____

_____

_____

On a piece of paper:

- draw or write what you would look like.
- describe what you would like to do.

After all have finished, fold your papers and place them in a container. Each member of the group takes a paper from the container, shows it to the group, and tries to guess the identity of the person described on it. Then have the person share with the group responses to the following questions:

- Why did you pick that person or thing?
- What does your choice tell others about you?

◀ JOURNAL ▶

Find a quiet place.
Think about the following questions:

- What importance or value do I see in my choice?
- What can I discover about myself from my choice?

Write your responses in the space below.

◀ SCRIPTURE REFLECTION ▶

Sometimes you might wonder what God really wants you to be and to do in your life. In the gospel, Jesus teaches that everything we do and say must show that we are trying to live the Law of Love. Listen carefully to what Jesus says.

Reader: A teacher of the Law tried to trap Jesus with a question. "Teacher," he asked, "which is the greatest commandment in the Law?"

Jesus answered, "Love the Lord your God with all your heart, with all your soul, and with all your mind. This is the greatest and the most important commandment. The second most important commandment is like it: Love your neighbor as you love yourself."

From Matthew 22:34–40

Imagine that you are one of Jesus' disciples. Later that evening you and the other disciples gather to discuss Jesus' response to the teacher of the Law. What might you say?

Take a few moments to think about the following:

● What does the Law of Love mean to me?

● What people do I know who are living the Law of Love? Tell how.

● What are the talents or the things that I do best?

● How can I use my talents to live the Law of Love?

◀ JOURNAL ▶

Reflect briefly on your responses in the group discussion.

Write your reflections here.

◀ GROUP DISCUSSION ▶

Divide into small groups and discuss your responses. Then choose a group leader to share your group's discussion with the larger group.

◀ AUDIO-VISUAL ▶
ACTIVITY

On the day of your Baptism, your parents and godparents promised to help you to live the Law of Love. Now you are taking more responsibility for living that promise. After watching a videotape or filmstrip on the sacrament of Baptism, take a few minutes to reflect individually on the following:

- How does the videotape or filmstrip help me to understand my Baptism?
- How does the Law of Love guide me to live the new life I received in Baptism?
- How does the Law of Love guide me to live as a member of the body of Christ, the Church?
- Share your reflections with your group.

◀ LIVING THE LAW ▶
OF LOVE

Divide into three groups. Each group will do one of the following projects.

- Create a word collage depicting the Law of Love.
- Illustrate a mural showing how you will live the Law of Love.
- Role-play a TV spot reporting on the Law of Love.

Each group will present its completed project during the closing prayer service.

◀ PRAYER SERVICE ▶

Opening Hymn

"They Will Know We Are Christians by Our Love" (or another appropriate hymn)

Scripture Reading

Reader: A reading from the holy gospel according to John.

Jesus said to His disciples, "My commandment is this: love one another, just as I love you. The greatest love people can have for friends is to give their life for them. I chose you and appointed you to go and bear much fruit, the kind of fruit that endures. This, then, is what I command you: love one another."

From John 15:11–17

Presentation of Projects

Each group presents and explains its project on the Law of Love.

Prayer of the Faithful

Leader: When we live our Baptism by following the Law of Love, we become signs of God's love and help bring about the reign of God. Today, we pray for the coming of the reign of God.

Prayer leader 1: For our pope, our bishop, our priests, and all who lead our Church in service and worship, we pray to the Lord.

All: Thy kingdom come; thy will be done. (Repeat this response after each petition.)

Prayer leader 2: For the leaders of our world, our nation, our state, and our communities, we pray to the Lord. (Response)

Prayer leader 3: For ourselves, that we may reach out to help the hungry, the homeless, those suffering from injustice, oppression, illness, or addiction, and for all those with special needs, we pray to the Lord. (Response)

Prayer leader 4: For the needs of those in our parish and neighborhood, especially…(Response)

Now quietly pray this prayer.

† Holy Spirit, help me to live my Baptism and follow the Law of Love by

_____

_____

_____ .

Amen.

◀ BLESSING ▶

Turn to a partner and trace a cross on her or his forehead, saying:

† As Christ was anointed priest, prophet, and king, so may you always live the Law of Love and bring about the reign of God.

Closing Hymn
"They Will Know We Are Christians by Our Love" (or another appropriate hymn)

Sharing Our Faith As Catholics

God is close to us at all times and in all places, calling us and helping us in coming to faith. When a person is baptized and welcomed into the faith community of the Church, everyone present stands with family and other members of the parish. We hear the words, "This is our faith. This is the faith of the Church. We are proud to profess it in Christ Jesus, our Lord." And we joyfully answer, "Amen"—"Yes, God, I believe."

The Catholic Church is our home in the Christian community. We are proud to be Catholics, living as disciples of Jesus Christ in our world. Each day we are called to share our faith with everyone we meet, helping to build up the reign of God.

What is the faith we want to live and to share? Where does the gift of faith come from? How do we celebrate it and worship God? How do we live it? How do we pray to God? In these pages, you will find a special faith guide written just for you. It can help you as a fifth grader to grow in your Catholic faith and to share it with your family and with others, too.

Following the Church's teachings and what God has told us in the Bible, we can outline some of our most important beliefs and practices in four ways:

WHAT WE BELIEVE—CREED

HOW WE CELEBRATE—SACRAMENTS

HOW WE LIVE—MORALITY

HOW WE PRAY—PRAYER

CATHOLICS BELIEVE...

THERE IS ONE GOD IN THREE DIVINE PERSONS: Father, Son, and Holy Spirit. One God in three divine Persons is called the Blessed Trinity; it is the central teaching of the Christian religion.

GOD THE FATHER is the creator of all things.

GOD THE SON took on human flesh and became one of us. This is called the incarnation. Our Lord Jesus Christ, who is the Son of God born of the Virgin Mary, proclaimed the reign of God. Jesus gave us the new commandment of love and taught us the way of the Beatitudes. We believe that by His sacrifice on the cross, He died to save us from the power of sin—original sin and our personal sins. He was buried and rose from the dead on the third day. Through His resurrection we share in the divine life, which we call grace. Jesus, the Christ, is our Messiah. He ascended into heaven and will come again to judge the living and the dead.

GOD THE HOLY SPIRIT is the third Person of the Blessed Trinity, adored together with the Father and Son. The action of the Holy Spirit in our lives enables us to respond to the call of Jesus to live as faithful disciples.

We believe in **ONE, HOLY, CATHOLIC, AND APOSTOLIC CHURCH** founded by Jesus on the "rock," which is Peter, and the other apostles.

As Catholics, **WE SHARE A COMMON FAITH.** We believe and respect what the Church teaches: everything that is contained in the word of God, both written and handed down to us.

We believe in **THE COMMUNION OF SAINTS** and that we are to live forever with God.

I have also learned this year that
to believe as a Catholic means

_____

_____

_____

CATHOLICS CELEBRATE...

THE CHURCH, THE BODY OF CHRIST, continues the mission of Jesus Christ throughout human history. Through the sacraments and by the power of the Holy Spirit, the Church enters into the mystery of the death and resurrection of the Savior and the life of grace.

THE SEVEN SACRAMENTS are Baptism, Confirmation, Eucharist, Holy Orders, Matrimony, Reconciliation, and Anointing of the Sick. Through the sacraments, we share in God's grace so that we may live as disciples of Jesus.

THE SACRAMENTS ARE EFFECTIVE SIGNS through which Jesus Christ shares God's life and love with us. Through the power of the Holy Spirit, they actually bring about what they promise.

The Church carries on Jesus' mission of welcoming members into the body of Christ when we celebrate Baptism, Confirmation, and Eucharist. We call these the sacraments of initiation.

The Church forgives and heals as Jesus did by celebrating Reconciliation and Anointing of the Sick. We call these the sacraments of healing.

The Church serves others and is a special sign of God's love by celebrating and living the sacraments of Matrimony and Holy Orders. We call these the sacraments of service.

IN THE SACRAMENTS, WE RECEIVE GOD'S GRACE: a sharing in the divine life, in God's very life and love. In the sacraments, Jesus shares God's life with the Church by the power of the Holy Spirit. Jesus calls us to respond by living as His disciples.

By celebrating the sacraments, the Church worships and praises God. In celebrating the sacraments, the Church becomes a powerful sign of Jesus' presence and God's reign in our world.

Catholics celebrate...

By participating in the celebration of the sacraments, Catholics grow in holiness and in living as disciples of Jesus. Freed from sin by Baptism and strengthened by Confirmation, we are nourished by Christ Himself in the Eucharist. We also share in God's mercy and love in the sacrament of Reconciliation.

CATHOLICS CELEBRATE THE EUCHARIST AT MASS. They do this together with a priest. The priest has received the sacrament of Holy Orders and acts in the person of Christ, our High Priest. The Mass is both a meal and a sacrifice. It is a meal because in the Mass Jesus, the Bread of Life, gives us Himself to be our food. Jesus is really present in the Eucharist. The Mass is a sacrifice, too, because we remember all that Jesus did for us to save us from sin and to bring us new life. In this great sacrifice of praise, we offer ourselves with Jesus to God.

THE EUCHARIST IS THE SACRAMENT OF JESUS' BODY AND BLOOD. It is the high point of Catholic worship. It is a great privilege to take part weekly in the celebration of the Mass with our parish community.

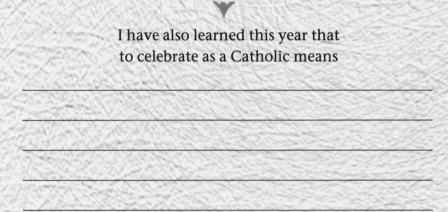

I have also learned this year that
to celebrate as a Catholic means

_____

_____

_____

_____

_____

CATHOLICS LIVE...

WE ARE MADE IN THE IMAGE AND LIKENESS OF GOD and are called to live as disciples of Jesus Christ. Jesus said to us, "Love one another as I have loved you."

When we live the way Jesus showed us and follow His teachings, we can be truly happy and live in real freedom.

To help us live as Jesus' disciples, we are guided by **THE LAW OF LOVE, THE BEATITUDES, AND THE TEN COMMANDMENTS.** The Works of Mercy and the Laws of the Church also show us how to grow in living as Jesus' disciples.

AS MEMBERS OF THE CHURCH, THE BODY OF CHRIST, we are guided by the Church's teachings that help us to form our conscience. These teachings have come down to us from the time of Jesus and the apostles and have been lived by God's people throughout history. We share them with millions of Catholics throughout the world.

THROUGH PRAYER AND THE SACRAMENTS, especially Eucharist and Reconciliation, we are strengthened to live as Jesus asked us to live. In faith, hope, and love, we as Catholic Christians are called not just to follow rules. We are called to live a whole new way of life as disciples of Jesus.

In living as Jesus' disciples, we are challenged each day to choose between right and wrong. Even when we are tempted to make wrong choices, the Holy Spirit is always present to help us make the right choices. Like Jesus, we are to live for God's reign. Doing all this means that we live a Christian moral life. As Christians we are always called to follow the way of Jesus.

I have also learned this year that
to live as a Catholic means

_____

_____

_____

CATHOLICS PRAY...

Prayer is talking and listening to God. We pray prayers of thanksgiving and sorrow; we praise God, and we ask God for what we need as well as for the needs of others.

We can pray in many ways and at any time. We can pray using our own words, words from the Bible, or just by being quiet in God's presence. We can also pray with song or dance or movement.

We also pray the prayers of our Catholic family that have come down to us over many centuries. Some of these prayers are the Our Father, the Hail Mary, the Glory to the Father, the Apostles' Creed, the Angelus, the Hail Holy Queen, and Acts of Faith, Hope, Love, and Contrition. Catholics also pray the rosary while meditating on events in the lives of Jesus and Mary.

As members of the Catholic community, we participate in the great liturgical prayer of the Church, the Mass. We also pray with the Church during the liturgical seasons of the Church year—Advent, Christmas, Lent, the Triduum, Easter, and Ordinary Time.

In prayer, we are joined with the whole communion of saints in praising and honoring God.

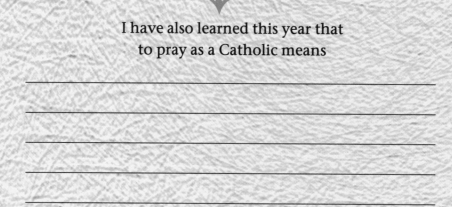

I have also learned this year that
to pray as a Catholic means

_____

_____

_____

_____

_____

By this time, you should know many of these prayers and practices by heart.

Sign of the Cross

In the name of the Father,
and of the Son,
and of the Holy Spirit. Amen.

Glory to the Father

Glory to the Father,
and to the Son,
and to the Holy Spirit:
as it was in the beginning,
is now, and will be for ever. Amen.

Our Father

Our Father, who art in heaven,
hallowed be thy name;
thy kingdom come;
thy will be done on earth
as it is in heaven.
Give us this day our daily bread;
and forgive us our trespasses
as we forgive those
who trespass against us;
and lead us not into temptation,
but deliver us from evil. Amen.

Hail Mary

Hail Mary, full of grace,
the Lord is with you;
blessed are you among women,
and blessed is the fruit
of your womb, Jesus.
Holy Mary, Mother of God,
pray for us sinners now
and at the hour of our death. Amen.

Morning Offering

My God, I offer you all my prayers, works, and sufferings of this day for all the intentions of your most Sacred Heart. Amen.

Evening Prayer

Dear God,
before I sleep
I want to thank you for this day,
so full of your kindness
and your joy.
I close my eyes to rest
safe in your loving care.

Grace Before Meals

Bless us, O Lord,
and these your gifts
which we are about to receive
from your bounty,
through Christ our Lord. Amen.

Grace After Meals

We give you thanks, almighty God,
for these and all your gifts
which we have received
through Christ our Lord. Amen.

Memorare

Remember, O most gracious Virgin Mary, that never was it known that anyone who fled to your protection, implored your help, or sought your intercession was left unaided. Inspired with this confidence, we fly unto you, O Virgin of virgins, our Mother. To you we come, before you we kneel, sinful and sorrowful. O Mother of the Word made flesh, do not despise our petitions, but in your mercy hear and answer them. Amen.

Apostles' Creed

I believe in God, the Father almighty,
creator of heaven and earth.

I believe in Jesus Christ,
his only Son, our Lord.
He was conceived by the power
of the Holy Spirit
and born of the Virgin Mary.
He suffered under Pontius Pilate,
was crucified, died, and was buried.
He descended to the dead.
On the third day he rose again.
He ascended into heaven,
and is seated at the right hand
of the Father.
He will come again to judge
the living and the dead.

I believe in the Holy Spirit,
the holy catholic Church,
the communion of saints,
the forgiveness of sins,
the resurrection of the body,
and the life everlasting. Amen.

Prayer to the Holy Spirit

Come, Holy Spirit,
fill the hearts of your faithful
and enkindle in them
the fire of your love.
Send forth your Spirit and
they shall be created, and
you shall renew the face of
the earth.

Nicene Creed

We believe in one God,
the Father, the Almighty,
maker of heaven and earth,
of all that is seen and unseen.

We believe in one Lord, Jesus Christ,
the only Son of God,
eternally begotten of the Father,
God from God, Light from Light,
true God from true God,
begotten, not made,
one in Being with the Father.
Through him all things were made.
For us men and for our salvation
he came down from heaven:
by the power of the Holy Spirit
he was born of the Virgin Mary,
and became man.

For our sake he was crucified
under Pontius Pilate;
he suffered, died, and was buried.
On the third day he rose again
in fulfillment of the Scriptures;
he ascended into heaven and is seated
at the right hand of the Father.
He will come again in glory
to judge the living and the dead,
and his kingdom will have no end.

We believe in the Holy Spirit,
the Lord, the giver of life,
who proceeds from the Father
and the Son.
With the Father and the Son
he is worshiped and glorified.
He has spoken through the Prophets.

We believe in one holy catholic
and apostolic Church.
We acknowledge one baptism
for the forgiveness of sins.
We look for the resurrection of the dead,
and the life of the world to come. Amen.

Act of Contrition

My God,
I am sorry for my sins with all my heart.
In choosing to do wrong
and failing to do good,
I have sinned against you
whom I should love above all things.
I firmly intend, with your help,
to do penance,
to sin no more,
and to avoid whatever leads me to sin.
Our Savior Jesus Christ
suffered and died for us.
In his name, my God, have mercy.

Prayer for My Vocation

Dear God,
You have a great and loving plan
for our world and for me.
I wish to share in that plan fully,
faithfully, and joyfully.

Help me to understand what it is
you wish me to do with my life.
Help me to be attentive to the signs
that you give me about preparing for the future.

Help me to learn to be a sign
of the kingdom, or reign, of
God whether I'm called to the
priesthood or religious life,
the single or married life.

And once I have heard and understood
your call, give me the strength
and the grace to follow it
with generosity and love. Amen.

The Angelus

The angel of the Lord declared to Mary
and she conceived by the Holy Spirit.
Hail Mary....

Behold the handmaid of the Lord,
be it done to me according to your word.
Hail Mary....

And the Word was made Flesh
and dwelled among us.
Hail Mary....

Pray for us, O Holy Mother of God,
That we may be worthy of the promises of
Christ.
Let us pray:
Pour forth, we beseech you, O Lord,
your grace into our hearts
that we to whom the incarnation of
Christ your Son was made known by the
message of an angel may,
by his passion and cross,
be brought to the glory of his resurrection,
through Christ Our Lord. Amen.

Prayer of Saint Francis

Lord, make me an instrument of your peace:
where there is hatred, let me sow love;
where there is injury, pardon;
where there is doubt, faith;
where there is despair, hope;
where there is darkness, light;
where there is sadness, joy.
O Divine Master, grant that I may not
so much seek
to be consoled as to console,
to be understood as to understand,
to be loved as to love.
For it is in giving that we receive,
it is in pardoning that we are pardoned,
and it is in dying that we are born
to eternal life.

The Stations of the Cross

1. Jesus is condemned to die.
2. Jesus takes up His cross.
3. Jesus falls the first time.
4. Jesus meets His Mother.
5. Simon helps Jesus carry His cross.
6. Veronica wipes the face of Jesus.
7. Jesus falls the second time.
8. Jesus meets the women of Jerusalem.
9. Jesus falls the third time.
10. Jesus is stripped of His garments.
11. Jesus is nailed to the cross.
12. Jesus dies on the cross.
13. Jesus is taken down from the cross.
14. Jesus is laid in the tomb.

Hail, Holy Queen

Hail, Holy Queen, Mother of Mercy;
hail, our life, our sweetness,
and our hope! To you do we cry,
poor banished children of Eve;
to you do we send up our sighs,
mourning and weeping in this valley of tears.

Turn, then, most gracious advocate,
your eyes of mercy toward us;
and after this our exile, show unto us
the blessed fruit of your womb, Jesus,
O clement, O loving, O sweet Virgin Mary!

The Rosary

A rosary has a cross, followed by one large bead and three small ones. Then there is a circle with five "decades." Each decade consists of one large bead followed by ten smaller beads. Begin the rosary with the sign of the cross. Recite the Apostles' Creed. Then pray one Our Father, three Hail Marys, and one Glory to the Father.

To recite each decade, say one Our Father on the large bead and ten Hail Marys on the ten smaller beads. After each decade, pray the Glory to the Father. As you pray each decade, think of the appropriate joyful, sorrowful, or glorious mystery, or a special event in the life of Jesus and Mary. Pray the Hail, Holy Queen as the last prayer of the rosary.

The Five Joyful Mysteries (by custom, used on Mondays, Thursdays, and the Sundays of Advent)

1. The annunciation
2. The visitation
3. The birth of Jesus
4. The presentation of Jesus in the Temple
5. The finding of Jesus in the Temple

The Five Sorrowful Mysteries
(by custom, used on Tuesdays, Fridays, and the Sundays of Lent)

1. The agony in the garden
2. The scourging at the pillar
3. The crowning with thorns
4. The carrying of the cross
5. The crucifixion and death of Jesus

The Five Glorious Mysteries
(by custom, used on Wednesdays, Saturdays, and the remaining Sundays of the year)

1. The resurrection
2. The ascension
3. The Holy Spirit comes upon the apostles
4. The assumption of Mary into heaven
5. The coronation of Mary in heaven

Prayer of Inner Stillness

Choose a time when you can be alone. Sit in a comfortable position and relax by breathing deeply. Try to shut out all the sights and sounds around you so that you feel the peaceful rhythm of your breathing in and out.

Slowly repeat a short prayer such as "Come, Lord Jesus" or perhaps just the name Jesus.

A Scripture Meditation

1. Pray for inner stillness.
2. Read one of your favorite stories about Jesus.
3. Close your eyes and imagine you are with Jesus.
4. Talk to Jesus about what the reading means to you.

The Storm at Sea

Quiet your mind and body as you breathe deeply.
Pray, "Jesus, be with me."

Listen to God's Word

One day Jesus got into a boat with His disciples. As they were sailing, Jesus fell asleep. Suddenly a strong wind came up, and the boat began to fill with water. They woke Jesus, saying, "Master, Master! We are about to die!"

Jesus got up and gave an order to the wind and to the stormy water. They quieted down, and there was great calm.

From Luke 8:22–24

Imagine you are in the boat with Jesus. What do you say to the other disciples when you first see the storm? What do you say to Jesus?

What do you say to yourself after Jesus calms the storm?

What are things that can cause storms in your life right now? Imagine Jesus is standing in front of you. Talk to Jesus about how you can become calm.

Decide how you can help others through stormy times.

Pray in these words or your own

Jesus, when a storm comes up in my life, calm my fears.

When I am afraid to do what I know is right, give me courage.

When I am afraid to try something new because I might fail, give me hope.

When I have a problem that is too big to handle alone, give me trust in You and in those who can help me.

The Ten Commandments

1. I am the Lord your God, who brought you out of slavery. Worship no god except Me.

2. You shall not misuse the name of the Lord your God.

3. Remember to keep holy the Sabbath day.

4. Honor your father and mother.

5. You shall not kill.

6. You shall not commit adultery.

7. You shall not steal.

8. You shall not tell lies against your neighbor.

9. You shall not want to take your neighbor's wife or husband.

10. You shall not want to take your neighbor's possessions.

The Beatitudes

Happy are the poor in spirit; the kingdom of God belongs to them!

Happy are those who mourn; God will comfort them!

Happy are those who are humble; they will receive what God has promised!

Happy are those who do what God wants; God will satisfy them fully!

Happy are those who are merciful to others; God will have mercy on them!

Happy are the pure in heart; they will see God!

Happy are those who work for peace; they will be called children of God!

Happy are those who are persecuted because they do what God wants; the kingdom of heaven belongs to them!

The Laws of the Church

1. Celebrate Christ's resurrection every Sunday (or Saturday evening) and on holy days of obligation by taking part in Mass and avoiding unnecessary work.

2. Lead a sacramental life. Receive Holy Communion frequently and the sacrament of Penance, or Reconciliation, regularly. We must receive Holy Communion at least once a year at Lent-Easter. We must confess within a year, if we have committed serious, or mortal, sin.

3. Study Catholic teaching throughout life, especially in preparing for the sacraments.

4. Observe the marriage laws of the Catholic Church and give religious training to one's children.

5. Strengthen and support the Church: one's own parish, the worldwide Church, and the Holy Father.

6. Do penance, including not eating meat and fasting from food on certain days.

7. Join in the missionary work of the Church.

Holy Days of Obligation

On these days Catholics must celebrate the Eucharist just as on Sunday.

1. Solemnity of Mary, Mother of God (Jan. 1)
2. Ascension (During the Easter season)
3. Assumption of Mary (August 15)
4. All Saints Day (November 1)
5. Immaculate Conception (December 8)
6. Christmas (December 25)

Corporal and Spiritual Works of Mercy (see page 173)

Absolution (page 105)

Absolution is the prayer the priest says asking forgiveness of our sins.

Anointing of the Sick (page 111)

The sacrament of Anointing of the Sick brings God's special blessings to those who are sick, elderly, or dying.

Apostles (page 149)

The apostles were the twelve special helpers chosen by Jesus to lead the early Church.

Ascension (page 33)

The ascension is the event in which Jesus Christ was taken into heaven after the resurrection.

Baptism (page 59)

Baptism is the sacrament of our new life with God and the beginning of our initiation into the Church. Through this sacrament we are freed from sin, become children of God, and are welcomed as members of the Church.

Beatitudes (page 208)

The Beatitudes are ways of living that Jesus gave us so that we can be truly happy.

Bethlehem (page 96)

The town in which Jesus was born.

Blessed Sacrament (page 73)

Another name for the Eucharist. Jesus is really present in the Blessed Sacrament.

Catholic (page 148)

The Church welcomes all people and has the message of God's good news for all people.

Confirmation (page 65)

Confirmation is the sacrament in which we are sealed with the gift of the Holy Spirit and are strengthened to give witness to the good news of Jesus.

Conscience (page 44)

Conscience is the ability we have to decide whether a thought, word, or deed is right or wrong. We form our conscience according to the teachings of the Church.

Consecration (page 77)

The consecration is that part of the Mass in which the bread and wine become Jesus' own Body and Blood through the power of the Holy Spirit and the words and actions of the priest.

Corporal Works of Mercy (page 173)

The Corporal Works of Mercy are ways we care for one another's physical needs.

Disciple (page 15)

A disciple is one who learns from and follows Jesus Christ.

Divine (page 14)

A word that means having the nature of God.

Eucharist (page 71)

The Eucharist is the sacrament of Jesus' Body and Blood. Jesus is really present in the Eucharist. Our gifts of bread and wine become the Body and Blood of Christ at Mass.

Evangelization (page 129)

Evangelization means spreading the good news of Jesus Christ and sharing our faith by our words and actions.

Faith (page 161)

Faith is a virtue that enables us to trust and believe in God, to accept what God has revealed, and to live according to God's loving will.

Fruits of the Holy Spirit (page 67)

The Fruits of the Holy Spirit are the good results people can see in us when we use the gifts of the Holy Spirit. They are love, joy, peace, patience, kindness, goodness, faithfulness, humility, and self-control.

Gifts of the Holy Spirit (page 65)

The seven gifts of the Holy Spirit are: wisdom, understanding, right judgment, courage, knowledge, reverence, and wonder and awe. They help us to live and witness to our Catholic faith.

Grace (page 39)

Grace is a sharing in the divine life, in God's very life and love.

Holy Orders (page 123)

Holy Orders is the sacrament that confers the ordained ministry of bishops, priests, and deacons.

Hope (page 167)

Hope is a virtue that enables us to trust that God will be with us in every situation.

Incarnation (page 17)

The incarnation is the mystery of God "becoming flesh," or becoming one of us in Jesus Christ.

Kingdom of Heaven (page 27)

The kingdom of heaven is another way of saying kingdom, or reign, of God in Matthew's gospel.

Laity (page 129)

The laity are single or married people who belong to the Church. Lay people serve the Church in many ways.

Law of Love (page 23)

Love the Lord your God with all your heart, with all your soul, with all your strength, and with all your mind. Love your neighbor as you love yourself.

Liturgical Year (page 82-83)

Advent, Christmas, Lent, the Easter Triduum, Easter, and Ordinary Time make up the seasons, or times, of the liturgical year. Our Church celebrates the liturgical year to help us remember the whole story of the life, death, and resurrection of Jesus Christ.

Liturgy (page 77)

Liturgy is the official public worship of the Church. The Liturgy includes the ways we celebrate the Mass and the other sacraments.

Liturgy of the Eucharist (page 76)

The Liturgy of the Eucharist is one of the two major parts of the Mass. It is made up of the Presentation and Preparation of the Gifts, the Eucharistic Prayer, and Holy Communion.

Liturgy of the Word (page 76)

The Liturgy of the Word is one of the two major parts of the Mass. It is made up of readings from the Old and New Testaments, Responsorial Psalm, Gospel, Homily, Creed, and Prayer of the Faithful.

Love (page 173)

Love is a virtue that enables us to love God, our neighbor, and ourselves.

Marks of the Church (page 148)

The marks of the Church are: one, holy, catholic, and apostolic. These are four great identifying qualities that let people know the kind of community Jesus began and calls us to be.

Mass (page 76)

The Mass is our celebration of the Eucharist. The two major parts of the Mass are the Liturgy of the Word and the Liturgy of the Eucharist.

Matrimony (page 117)

The sacrament of Matrimony is a powerful and effective sign of Christ's presence that joins a man and woman together for life.

Messiah (page 88)

"Messiah" refers to the savior and liberator promised to the people in the Old Testament. Jesus is the Messiah.

Original Sin (page 61)

Original sin is the first sin of humankind. Every human being is born with and suffers from the effects of this sin.

Passover (page 70)

Passover is a feast in which Jews celebrate God's deliverance of their ancestors from slavery in Egypt.

Penance (page 105)

The penance we receive from the priest in the sacrament of Reconciliation helps to make up for the hurt caused by our sins and helps us to avoid sin in the future. Our penance can be a prayer or good deed.

Pope (page 149)

The pope is the bishop of Rome. He is the successor of Saint Peter and the leader of the whole Catholic Church.

Prayer (page 202)

Prayer is directing one's heart and mind to God. In prayer we talk and listen to God.

Priesthood of the Faithful (page 128)

The priesthood of the faithful is the priesthood of Jesus in which all baptized people share through Baptism and the anointing of the Holy Spirit.

Racism (page 155)

Racism is a sin of prejudice against a person because of race.

Reconciliation (page 104)

Reconciliation is the sacrament in which we are forgiven by God and the Church for our sins.

Reign of God (Kingdom of God) (page 21)

The reign, or kingdom, of God is the saving power of God's life and love in the world.

Sacrament (page 39)

A sacrament is an effective sign through which Jesus Christ shares God's life and love with us. The sacraments cause to happen the very things they stand for. There are seven sacraments.

Sacramental (page 178)

A sacramental is a blessing, an action, or an object that helps us remember God, Jesus, Mary, or the saints.

Sin (page 105)

Sin is freely choosing to do what we know is wrong. When we sin, we disobey God's law on purpose.

Spiritual Works of Mercy (page 173)

The Spiritual Works of Mercy are ways we care for one another's spiritual needs.

Ten Commandments (page 208)

The Ten Commandments are laws given to us by God to help us live as God's people. God gave the Ten Commandments to Moses on Mount Sinai.

Viaticum (page 113)

When Holy Communion is given to a dying person, it is called Viaticum. Viaticum means "food for the journey." Viaticum is often received along with the sacrament of Anointing of the Sick.

Vocation (page 128)

A vocation is our call to live holy lives of service in our Church and in our world.

Worship (page 39)

Worship is praise and thanks to God in signs, words, and actions.

INDEX

*****Bold-faced** pages indicate chapters

†*Italics* refer to definitions

Bold-faced pages indicate chapters

†*Italics* refer to definitions

Answers for Reviews

Lesson 1 (pg. 18): **1.** c **2.** b **3.** a **4.** d
Lesson 2 (pg. 24): **1.** c **2.** b **3.** d **4.** c
Lesson 3 (pg. 30): **1.** c **2.** b **3.** d **4.** a
Lesson 4 (pg. 36): **1.** c **2.** b **3.** b **4.** d
Lesson 5 (pg. 42): **1.** b **2.** c **3.** d **4.** b
Lesson 6 (pg. 48): **1.** forgive sins in His name. **2.** the sacrament of Reconciliation. **3.** when we are sorry. **4.** making an examination of conscience.
Lesson 7 (pg. 54): **1.** c **2.** a **3.** c **4.** b
Unit 1 (pg. 56): **1.** c **2.** d **3.** b **4.** a **5.** c
Lesson 8 (pg. 62): **1.** b **2.** b **3.** d **4.** a
Lesson 9 (pg. 68): **1.** d **2.** a **3.** c **4.** d
Lesson 10 (pg. 74): **1.** d **2.** a **3.** c **4.** b
Lesson 11 (pg. 80): **1.** c **2.** b **3.** a **4.** d
Lesson 12 (pg. 86): **1.** a **2.** d **3.** b **4.** c
Lesson 13 (pg. 92): **1.** Immanuel **2.** Mother of the Savior **3.** light **4.** wise and just
Lesson 14 (pg. 98): **1.** F **2.** T **3.** F **4.** T
Summary 1 (pg. 101-102): **1.** c **2.** a **3.** c **4.** b **5.** d **6.** initiation **7.** healing

8. service **9.** Holy Spirit **10.** Body and Blood *In 11–20, cross out:* **11.** holy water **12.** our citizenship **13.** holy oil **14.** need help to live **15.** ordinary bread and wine **16.** the Ascension **17.** His ascension into heaven **18.** Christmas **19.** Ash Wednesday **20.** Good Friday
Lesson 15 (pg. 108): **1.** 2, 5, 1, 4, 3 **2.** b **3.** b **4.** c
Lesson 16 (pg. 114): **1.** b **2.** d **3.** a **4.** c
Lesson 17 (pg. 120): **1.** love. **2.** Be true at all times and love one another forever. **3.** His Church. **4.** God's love for the world.
Lesson 18 (pg. 126): **1.** apostles **2.** Bishops **3.** deacons **4.** laying on of hands
Lesson 19 (pg. 132): **1.** F, T, T **2.** vocation **3.** the priesthood of the faithful **4.** evangelization
Lesson 20 (pg. 138): **1.** d **2.** b **3.** a **4.** b
Lesson 21 (pg. 144): **1.** the Mass of the Lord's Supper **2.** and remember the

Lord's Passion **3.** and our new life in Christ **4.** Easter Triduum
Unit 3 (pg. 146): **1.** b **2.** c **3.** d **4.** c **5.** b **6.** b **7.** a **8.** the Individual Rite and Communal Rite. **9.** through the sacraments of Reconciliation and Anointing of the Sick
Lesson 22 (pg. 152): **1.** one **2.** holy **3.** catholic **4.** apostolic
Lesson 23 (pg. 158): **1.** F (no circumstance) **2.** F (All Christians) **3.** T **4.** T
Lesson 24 (pg. 164): **1.** b **2.** c **3.** d **4.** c
Lesson 25 (pg. 170): **1.** a **2.** d **3.** b **4.** d
Lesson 26 (pg. 176): **1.** b **2.** d **3.** c **4.** a
Lesson 27 (pg. 182): **1.** Holy water **2.** crucifix **3.** Paschal Candle or Easter Candle **4.** ashes
Summary 2 (pg. 189-190): **1.** b **2.** c **3.** c **4.** a **5.** d **6.** contrition **7.** Sin **8.** lifelong **9.** bishops **10.** priests **11.** pope **12.** Jewish **13.** Trinity **14.** hope **15.** 7, 1, 6, 4, 8, 2, 3, 5

Acknowledgments

Grateful acknowledgment is due the following for their work on the New Edition of Coming to God's Life:

Mary Ann Trevaskiss, Project Editor
Kathleen Hlavacek, Editor
Tresse De Lorenzo, Manager: Production/Art
Joe Svadlenka, Art Director
Barbara Berger, Design Manager
Ana Jouvin, Designer

Excerpts and adaptations from *Good News Bible*, copyright © American Bible Society 1966, 1971, 1976, 1979.

Excerpts from the English translation of *Rite of Baptism for Children* © 1969, International Committee on English in the Liturgy, Inc. (ICEL); excerpts from the English translation of *The Roman Missal* © 1973, ICEL; excerpts from the English translation of *Rite of Penance* © 1974, ICEL; excerpts from the English translation of *Rite of Confirmation*, Second Edition, © 1975, ICEL; excerpts from the English translation of *Rite of Marriage* © 1969, ICEL; excerpts from *Pastoral Care of the Sick: Rites of Anointing and Viaticum* © 1982, ICEL. All rights reserved.

Photo Research

Jim Saylor

Cover Photos

Myrleen Cate: insets.
H. Armstrong Roberts: background and nature insets.

Photo Credits

Diane J. Ali: 12 left, 81 top, 184–185, 179 bottom center.
Animals Animals/Marcia W. Griffin: 57 left.
Art Resource, NY: 38–39; Scala: 82, 160, 166 left.
Dennis Barnes: 116.
Myrleen Cate: 7 top, 7 bottom, 10, 12 center left, 12 center right, 13, 27, 33, 34, 44, 45, 50, 50–51, 60, 65, 78 bottom, 81 center left, 81 bottom, 105, 109, 121, 128, 133 top, 165 bottom, 174, 147 top right, 147 bottom left, 153, 166 top right, 178, 178–179, 179 bottom right, 181, 191, 192, 194, 207.
CNS/Blimp Photo Company: 148–149; Arturo Mari: 148.
Bill Coleman: 155 right.
CROSIERS/Gene Plaisted, OSC: 64, 76, 94, 110, 123, 129, 141 center, 177, 179 bottom left, 180, 212.
Kathy Ferguson: 49.
FPG International/Ron Chapple: 61; Color Box: 63.
Christopher Talbot Frank: 57 right.
Nicholas H. Hemmer: 12 bottom.
Profiles West/Allen Russell: 147 left.
Frances M. Roberts: 111 left.
H. Armstrong Roberts: 29, 97, 103, 117 top, 134–135, 137, 141 top, 141 bottom, 167 top, 167 bottom.
Nancy Sheehan: 58, 66, 77, 78 top, 140, 196.
The Stock Market/Paul Barton: 7 center; Paul Chauncey: 57 top; Peter Beck: 59, 104, 118, 133 bottom; Bo Zaunders: 79; Jean Miele: 88–89; Anthony Edgeworth: 115.
Tony Stone Images/Paul Berger: 12 right; Rosemary Weller: 81 center right; Bob Torrez: 111 right; Dale Durfee: 117 bottom; Bill Aron: 154; David H. Endersbee: 165 background; David Olsen: 167 background.
H. Mark Weidman: 155 left.

Illustrators

Blaine Martin: Cover, Digital Imaging
Wendy Pierson: Cover, Logo Rendering
Skip Baker: 163, 168.
Jim Baldwin: 124, 125.
David Barber: 96.
David Barnett: 8–9, 20.
Karen Bell: 46, 90, 142.
Teresa Berasi: 161.
Lisa Blackshear: 35.
Robert Burger: 157.
Kevin Butler: 23, 105, 107, 119, 133, 135.
Young Sook Cho: 82–83.
Gwen Connelly: 58–59.
Neverne Covington: 26–27.
Daniel DelValle: 11, 53, 131.
Pat Dewitt: 183, 186.
Cathy Diefendorf: 75, 94–95, 156.
Victor Durango: 84.
Bill Farnsworth: 69.
Yvonne Gilbert: 87.
Adam Gordon: 12, 16, 17, 28, 29, 32, 33, 34, 39, 72, 73, 78, 79, 81, 85, 96, 97, 110, 118, 143, 171, 173, 179.
Brad Hamann: 41, 174.
John Haysom: 14–15, 70–71, 172.
Robert Jones: 151.
Ana Jouvin: 177.
Al Leiner: 122–123.
Judy Love: 25, 37, 106, 109.
Blaine Martin: 136, 162.
Shelley Matheis: 171.
Verlin Miller: 150.
Andrew Muonio: 113.
Cheryl Kirk Noll: 112.
Julie Pace: 184–185.
Julie Peterson: 51.
Wendy Pierson: 148–149.
Rodica Prato: 103.
Alan Reingold: 16, 17.
Dorothy Reinhardt: 76–77, 116–117.
Frank Riccio: 63.
Margaret Sanfilippo: 32, 33, 93, 127, 130, 139.
Joanne Scribner: 43.
Bob Shein: 19, 52, 91.
Mark Sparacio: 65, 67, 97, 115.
Tom Sperling: 31, 49, 134–135, 159.
Nancy Tobin: 175.
Gregg Valley: 22, 94–95.
Dean Wilhite: 128–129.
Jenny Williams: 40, 72.